FO

Thousands of books have been written on marriage. There are all kinds describing all kinds of marriage problems but most of them leave you cold! ...And with the same problems as you had before.

I have never read a book as cleverly written as *The Man of Her Dreams/The Woman of His!* This book puts into a nutshell the answer to every problem in every marriage. It is so simple, so easy to read and yet so totally challenging if you are having problems in your marriage.

Even if you are not having problems in your marriage, it can be a supernatural blessing.

We would recommend that you read this book and give a copy of it to every married friend you have.

Charles and Frances Hunter

"We rejoice for the help that this book will give people wanting a better marriage."

Pastor Billy Joe Daugherty
Victory Christian Center, Tulsa, Oklahoma

"I believe that *"The Man of Her Dreams/The Woman of His!"* is the best book on marriage that I have ever read. It is a tremendous book that is a work of the Holy Spirit, totally inspired by God. Every Pastor should have several copies on hand."

Dr. Richard Sigmund
Author: A Place Called Heaven

"I am very pleased at the approach Joel and Kathy take in *"The Man of Her Dreams/The Woman of His!"* It's real people with real answers. I am using it with my clients and I highly recommend its use to other professional marriage counselors."

Lisa Winchell, Licensed Pastoral Counselor

"The grace of God is very evident in the lives of Joel and Kathy. The Davissons became part of our new church family in 1991. Only a miracle could have saved their marriage back then. God gave them that miracle through His Word and their tenacious determination to prevail. Now, their insights shared through *The Man of Her Dreams/The Woman of His!* will surely help preserve other marriages needing help."

Pastors Jim & Pam Dumont
Erie Christian Fellowship Church, Erie, Pennsylvania

"My wife Sandi and I married in our teens. God by His grace has helped us to enjoy a dream life together. If the story and principles in this book can direct even one couple to dreams fulfilled, it will be a plus in a 'marriage world' that has too many sad endings. The first twenty-five years are the hardest, so to anyone who reads this book, I say 'don't give up.'"

Pastor Jerry Barnard
International Christian Center, Daytona Beach, Florida

"You are holding onto dynamite! If your marriage has reached the bottom of an ugly pit, hang on! It can change. There is hope! Let the application of biblical principles transform your marriage into the joyous, fulfilling experience that God intended!"

Elizabeth Jameison, Retired American Baptist Pastor

PREFACE

By Paul Hegstrom, Ph.D.

I remember Joel in the sessions at Life Skills. He was in a real blame game. Questions and challenges came! "What about her?" "When does this program deal with the wife?" "If she would get her life straight I would be okay!" The barrage of denial came fast and furious. I tried to be nice but that did not work so I had to directly confront the whole situation.

I became extremely firm and felt total resistance. I made the statement, "The wife is the responder and the husband is the activator so own your behavior and your attitude." As time went by, Joel's resistance did not decrease and his anger seemed to increase.

After the seminar was concluded, Kathy called me and we talked it out. I just knew Joel had tremendous potential if he ever got the truth of the Life Skills message. Well, it happened! He got it! The gracious God we serve used the truth to bring permanent change.

Change takes time. I told Joel that three years is average for change to grip our spirit. At that time three years was an eternity in Joel's mind, yet God's principles worked. You must read this book about Joel and Kathy's recovery. This book has a happy ending. Joel and Kathy, God will bless your message because of your transparency. Reader, you will be blessed also by the truth.

Life Skills International
Aurora, Colorado
(303) 340-0598
www.lifeskillsintl.org

From Joel and Kathy: In 1994, our marriage was in shambles. We attended Life Skills International in Aurora, Colorado, under the guise of being trained to be facilitators at an LSI Center. Our pastor at the time felt helpless in the face of our situation and arranged the trip. Paul, not realizing that we were brought for healing instead of training, commented in exasperation that this particular group of potential facilitators was the most needy that he had ever attempted to train in the history of Life Skills!

The Man Of Her Dreams/The Woman Of His!

Published by Joel and Kathy™
Copyright 2004, 2005, 2006, 2008 by Joel and Kathy™
All Rights Reserved.

Over 15,000 in print!

1st Edition		September 2004
2nd Edition		November 2004
3rd Edition	First Printing	April 2005
3rd Edition	Second Printing	November 2006
4th Edition		March 2008

E-mail your testimony, questions and comments to:
JoelandKathy4@aol.com and JoelandKathy@JoelandKathy.com
Visit us on the web at www.joelandkathy.com

Additional copies may be obtained by sending $15.00 plus $3.00 postage to:
Joel and Kathy Davisson
244 Pine Grove Drive
Palm Coast, Florida 32164
1-888-772-2331 or 386-206-3128

Volume Discounts
Orders of 40+ copies are offered at a 40% discount or more;
Prices do not include shipping:

20-39 copies	$10.00 each
40-119 copies	$9.00 each
120-499 copies	$8.00 each
500-999 copies	$7.00 each
Over 1000 copies	$6.00 each

Other Titles

Livin' It and Lovin' It (The Man of Her Dreams/The Woman of His! Part 2)	
9 CD Audio Book	$55
Paperback, 376 pages	$17
8-Hour DVD Seminar-The Man of Her Dreams/The Woman of His!	$50
4 CD Audio Book- The Man of Her Dreams/The Woman of His!	$35
The Making of a Ministry… Thoughts From the Throne	$7
Your Inherited Salvation Benefits Package	$7
How to Activate & Maintain the Blessings of God in Your Life	$9

Cover illustration and design by Mike Flipp: flippster@mchsi.com

ISBN 0-9766388-1-9 The Man of Her Dreams/The Woman of His!

The Man
Of Her Dreams

UPDATED FOR 2008!

The Woman
Of His!

Joel and Kathy

*Husband and Wife
Lovers, Parents,
Pastors, Friends*

Photography by Brian Pike Photography

ABOUT THE AUTHORS

Joel and Kathy share the Word of God as a unique ministry team. They flow together harmoniously as they share the Word of God and the principles of marriage restoration that they live. Their ministry brings life, strength and encouragement. The Word that God spoke to Joel in 1983 is now coming to pass: "You and Kathy will be married and I will touch many through you as a couple."

The ministry is a family affair. Joining Joel and Kathy in leading praise and worship, special music presentations, dance, healing the sick (and in baseball!) are their four young people: Chris (19), Jenifer (18), Josiah (14), and Shekinah (13).

Joel and Kathy emphasize family relationships and believe that ministry flows out of both successful husband and wife relationships and successful relationships with the children. Joel and Kathy minister a strong word of marriage restoration drawn from their years of struggle and the victory they now live. Joel and Kathy's unique "Weekend Marriage Intensives" bring miracles to worst case marriages.

DVD Seminar, Audio Book
Livin' It and Lovin' It!
Joel and Kathy offer an 8-hour DVD seminar and Audio Books of *The Man of Her Dreams/The Woman of His!* and part 2 - *Livin' It and Lovin' It!* Both are available at *www.godsavemymarriage.com*

Special Thanks to Elizabeth, Joel's mother, for the many hours that she dedicated to editing, critiquing and proofreading the first and second editions. You are an inspiration and a blessing to us.

Heidi L. Rau: We are so grateful that we met you at the Houston Astrodome. Thank you for the many hours that you spent helping us upgrade this third edition with your wonderful additional editing, formatting and fabulous suggestions. Your skill and selfless dedication are so greatly appreciated.

Paul and Judy Hegstrom: We thank God that you paid the price of restoration in your marriage and are presenting the principles that you learned through your ministry at Life Skills International.

Charles and Frances Hunter: Thank you for sharing your secrets of passion and love in marriage and for teaching us to minister in the supernatural. Thank you for renewing our wedding vows on our 20th anniversary at the Houston Astrodome. Finally, thank you so very, very, much for the wonderful foreword you have written for this book. We are so glad you liked it! You are truly awesome examples of what it means to serve the Lord with 100% dedication.

Pastors James and Pam Dumont of Erie Christian Fellowship: Thanks for being there for Kathy to call upon in times of need in that critical first year. Your support and affirmation of the call upon our lives gave us courage to press on. Your encouragement for us to focus exclusively on recovery as a family was a Word from God.

Roger Pugh: Your obedience in 1991 became an anchor. We had just stepped out of full time ministry to pursue family restoration. Your prophetic words were, "You will be a father and you will be a mother in the Body of Christ. If the Lord has His way in your life you will be in full time ministry." God has indeed had His way in us.

Pastors Gordon and Marilyn Shoemaker: That trip to Life Skills International saved our life!

Dedication

To Chris, Jenifer, Josiah and Shekinah, our four wonderful, unique, talented, sweet, loving and energetic young people! Our love for each of you grows more every day. You will be good husbands and wives or you will have us to deal with!

TABLE OF CONTENTS

INTRODUCTION

Wow! Guess What? If you are holding this book right now you are holding onto dynamite! Wait... don't drop it! Remember dynamite is often used to explode old, ugly buildings so that something of practicality and beauty may be built in its place. The principles of *The Man of Her Dreams, The Woman of His!* may shatter your "cemented" ideas. They may cause you to re-think your values. They may irritate you, they may tickle your funny bone, they may bring some tears. Just know that whatever stage of marriage you are experiencing, it really can get better. It can become wonderful. If you are happy, happy, happy in your relationship, give thanks. There's always room for "more happy!" You'll find it by using the principles expressed in this book. If your marriage has reached the bottom of an ugly pit, hang on! It can change. There is hope. If you're somewhere in the dull, boring, "in between" you are ready for a treat. It's time for an explosion into joy.

The Man of Her Dreams, The Woman of His! is not just words, theory or educational facts. It is life experience. It is the honest (very honest) exposure of the reality of a marriage on the rocks, in the rocks, under the rocks, crushed by the rocks. It is the story of a toxic, ugly relationship made beautiful by the dynamite explosions of the old and the building of the new. It is the story of my son. It is the story of my daughter-in-law. Nothing is held back. I am very proud of Joel and Kathy – my kids! I have been extremely blessed to see them grow into one of the most fulfilled couples I know.

Sixteen years ago I saw the marriage as very sad, dysfunctional and hopeless. It has been a miracle brought about by Joel and Kathy actually believing and working out the marriage principles of *The Man of Her Dreams, The Woman of His!*

Joel and Kathy made a choice. Today you are given that choice. For each of you it will be different. For some it will be to stay in the boring ho-hum of your relationship. For some it will be to stay in a trapped, abusive situation. For some it will be satisfaction with a marriage that seems as OK as the next. I trust that many of you will choose to open the doors of your hearts and minds – let the dynamite of God's power and the application of biblical principles transform your marriage into the joyous, fulfilling experience that God intended.

By Elizabeth Jameison,
Retired American Baptist Pastor

The Man of Her Dreams/Woman of His! *put the icing on the cake of our already good marriage! We are now living a **dream** marriage! When Doug and I got married 26 years ago we were born-again, committed Christians, earnestly seeking God's will for our lives. Shortly after marrying, though, it all fell apart. Between babies, bills and business our marriage deteriorated to the point that I wanted a divorce. In 1999 Doug attended a conference which resulted in his recommitting his life to the Lord. He came home a changed man. I had a new husband. It was very pleasant for 6 years as we communicated in healthy ways, treating each other with respect and dignity. This was wonderful – but little did I realize how great it could be! Doug read your book in 2005 and began to treat me like a queen. Here are some examples:*

When Doug comes home from work, he often asks me if there is anything that I would like to talk about. After I share my heart, he asks me if there is anything else. He listens and lets me know how glad he is for me to share whatever it is that I feel like sharing. I feel like I am in heaven.

Our daughter got married last month... During the entire trip and wedding preparations Doug could not have been more loving and attentive. He knew and met my needs even before I was aware of them myself.

A few months ago, we spent a few days at a resort. We reached a new level in our relationship... it was awesome being together, just focusing on having fun and being in love. Just like with God, there's no limit to the level of intimacy and closeness you can achieve when both parties are giving and loving and enjoying each other. We are like two teenagers in love after 26 years of marriage. Every day gets better. Thank you for putting the fun back into our marriage through your book. Doug and Kelley Matton, FL

Jenifer, Shekinah, Joel, Kathy, Josiah, Chris

Photography by Brian Pike Photography

Chapter One

All Of The Answers Lie In This One Question:

How Do I Become The Man That God Has Called Me To Be?

It was 1979. I was in solitary confinement for aiding and abetting in an armed robbery. I was 17.

I was a drug addict. I could not speak clearly from their effects. I had no hope.

I asked Jesus into my heart. I gave Him my life.

My Prayer?
"Lord, make me into the man that You created me to be."

I had no idea how He would answer that prayer.

When wisdom enters your heart and **knowledge is pleasant to your soul,** *discretion will preserve you;* **understanding will keep you.**
Proverbs 2:10-11

Authors' note: Throughout this book, certain words in scriptural citations have been bolded for emphasis.

On April 1, 1972, the pastor of a local church left his wife a letter. In the letter, the pastor outlined how she should handle the children, how she should handle the finances and what her first actions should be to minimize the damage to the church and household. He had been involved in an affair and was leaving her to be with the other woman, who had been his wife's best friend.

Nineteen years later, on April 1, 1991, another pastor left his wife a letter. In the letter, he outlined how she should handle the children, how she should handle the finances, and what her first actions should be to minimize the damage to the church and household. He had been involved in an affair and was leaving her to be with the other woman, who had been his wife's best friend.

The first pastor was my father. I was ten years old when he divorced my mother. I had no information regarding the day he left. I had no information regarding the letter he wrote. All I knew was my dad was a pastor who had divorced my mother when I was ten years old.

The second pastor, who left his wife 19 years later, was me! When my mother read the letter I had left for Kathy, she told me it was déjà vu. The letter I had left for

Kathy was virtually identical to the one my dad had left for her 19 years ago, to the day.

Although the stories began identically, they are unfolding differently. My father and my mother divorced and went their separate ways. Kathy and I, however, remained married – and in October of 2004 we celebrated the 20th anniversary of our marriage by renewing our wedding vows on stage at the Houston Astrodome during an historic evening when Charles and Frances Hunter led their final Healing Explosion.

More than 30,000 people had come from throughout the country to be a part of this historic evening and receive healing from the ministry of the Hunters and the healing teams that had been trained to minister healing to the sick. Joining us on stage for the ceremony were many of our heroes of the faith, including Rodney and Adonica Howard-Browne, Norvel Hayes, Marilyn and Wallace Hickey, Nick Pappas and Joan Hunter. Jaci Velasquez sang. It was an overwhelming experience and a dream come true for us.

We are not just married. We are outrageously happy. We are pastoring a wonderful church. We have four wonderful children who presently are between the ages of 13 and 19. We are madly in love with each other. I have become the man of her dreams and she surely is the woman of mine.

A question begs to be answered – a question that lies at the very heart of this book: My mother and father were divorced. Kathy and I were restored. What did we do differently than they did? For that matter, why do more than 80% of couples in ministry end up divorced in the wake of adultery rather than being restored? Why do so many couples simply endure a mostly dreary marriage, even if they never faced adultery or other major problem? What have we done to give us such a happy marriage, while so many others are simply surviving?

This book is dedicated to communicating the principles we have learned and have been living for more than ten years. Thanks to these principles, we have developed an outrageously happy marriage.

Throughout this book we will be fully transparent in describing our problems and how we overcame them. For even without the adultery, we had serious issues. Adultery was just a symptom of much deeper issues we were dealing with – issues that most married couples wrestle with at one level or another. If we can have a dream marriage after our severe relationship problems, you certainly can, too. The solutions that we found will heal your relationship, just as they healed ours.

Kathy is the woman of my dreams. She is a godly woman, she ministers by my side in our pastorate, and she is a fabulous mother. She looks out for all my needs. She even brings me coffee in the morning. Kathy is beautiful and she is very, very sexy.

How Could I Have Fallen Into Adultery?

There are many contributing factors leading to adultery; including the power of sin, deception and demonic influence. Sheer stupidity ranks right up there too!

All of these influences were involved; however, the purpose of this book is not to teach on demonic influence.

> **I WAS A PAWN IN SOME MASTER SCHEME OF THE ENEMY TO DESTROY OUR MARRIAGE, INFLICT PAIN UPON OUR CHILDREN AND ERASE THE POSSIBILITY OF OUR NEXT CHILDREN EVER BEING BORN.**

It is apparent that I was a pawn in some master scheme of the enemy to destroy our marriage, to inflict pain upon our first two children, to erase the possibility of our third and fourth children ever being born and to destroy our fruitful ministries. The demonic pressures that were upon me, culminating in my leaving Kathy on April 1, 1991, were indescribable.

Had I realized it was April 1, I would not have chosen that day simply because it was April Fool's Day. Satan's manipulation of two men – my father in 1972 and me in 1991 – on this particular day, testifies to the delight that Satan takes in making fools of those whom he convinces to walk even for a moment in his will.

The purpose of this book is not to elaborate on the power of sin to deceive, although I surely discovered the ability of sin to completely and utterly deceive a believer.

I entered into sin willingly. After that, I was overcome by its power. I thought I could get away with it. I thought I could control it. I thought I could "take a break" from my commitment to God and to my wife, dive into sin as if I were diving into a swimming pool – then climb out, dry off and pick up right where I had left off.

Not only was I acting under the power of deception, I was living in complete denial.

Sin takes you further than you intend to go, keeps you longer than you intend to stay, and costs you more than you intend to pay. The deception is that you are in control. You say to yourself, "God won't mind. He will forgive. If I am really careful, no one will ever know!"

The purpose of this book is not to teach on the power of intensive prayer. There was indeed a lot of intensive prayer on that fateful April day. Kathy prayed, the other husband prayed and everyone else who knew what was going on prayed. The fact that we came back to our spouses after only 24 hours is not a testimony to any virtue or strength of character on our parts. It is purely a testimony to the power of prayer.

How encouraging it is to see that the power of prayer was able to break the power of deception from two individuals who were ready to ruin their own lives along with many other people's lives. They came to their senses just enough to tuck their tails between their legs and make one step toward undoing the worst mistake of their lives.

As expected, the road has been long and challenging for both couples involved. The good news is that they have repaired their marriages and are living happily ever after... separated by hundreds of miles.

What does geographical location have to do with it? Logic may suggest that if both parties have repented, their proximity to one another would be irrelevant. But this is an illusion.

The reality is this: We have not met a minister who fell into adultery and was successfully restored while living in close proximity to the person they committed adultery with. To our knowledge, in every case in which neither party moved far away, divorces ultimately resulted. Although the offending minister returned back to his or her spouse in an attempt at restoration, the affair resumed within weeks or months – this time resulting in divorce.

Kathy and I have been successful in our restoration. Our experience trumps theory. We moved. Our restoration was successful and it has held for seventeen years. We have been exponentially, outrageously happy for the last fourteen of those 17 years.

Thankfully, this book is not a story about the power of adultery to bring a minister down. Yes, the sin of adultery is powerful one. It respects no person and it knows no bounds. The fact that during the course of ministry Kathy and I had prayed and laid hands on individuals and through the grace of God they were healed of cancer, brain tumor, scoliosis, blind eyes, crossed eyes, deaf ears, bad backs and many other medical conditions did not make me immune from entering into sin.

The fact that in the years before I had entered into adultery, Kathy and I had led a street ministry that had won hundreds of souls to the Lord did not keep me pure. The fact that we had daily prayer in our church, conducted miracle services in public places and had distributed some 40,000 pieces of gospel literature during the previous three years did not enable me to say "No" to my character flaw.

Astoundingly, the fact that we had seen God do various remarkable miracles in individual's lives, individuals who called us their pastors did not immunize me from falling. The fact that we tried very hard to have a loving relationship and the fact that we had two wonderful children did not keep me walking the straight and narrow.

You might find yourself wondering, "With all of this going for you, how could you fall? If **you** fell, what hope is there for **me?** Is there a solution?"

Yes, there is a solution. The solution is spelled out in the pages of this book.

We read about the failures of some of our highest-level leaders in *Charisma Magazine* – and in the daily press for that matter. All these, though, represent only the tip of the iceberg. There are many more hundreds, if not thousands, of nameless and faceless failures among ministers living in small hamlets, mid-sized towns and major metropolitan areas through out this country. We will never see and hear their stories on "60 Minutes."

Moving from the pulpit to the pews, we shudder to contemplate some of the goings on that are transpiring in the homes of tens of millions of everyday believers who are not in public ministry. There is one inescapable conclusion: There is something terribly wrong hidden in the recesses of men's hearts and behind the closed doors in homes throughout America.

As is always the case, the demonic deception and influence that resulted in my committing adultery did not affect me alone. The enemy's ultimate plan was to destroy our marriage, our family, and our ministries. Instead, by the grace of our Lord Jesus Christ, what the enemy intended for our destruction created the circumstances by which I came to realize there were deeper issues in play - issues that resulted in this public exposure of my character flaws.

> **THE ADULTERY MADE ME FACE THESE DEEPER ISSUES THAT, IF LEFT UNCHECKED, WOULD HAVE SENTENCED KATHY AND ME TO A LIFE-LONG MARRIAGE THAT WOULD HAVE BEEN MEDIOCRE AT BEST.**

The adultery made me face these deeper issues, which, if left unchecked, would have sentenced Kathy and me to a life-long marriage that would have been mediocre at best. We struggled for three painful years after the adultery before we received the knowledge that was needed for us to find complete healing.

We made an arduous journey of discovery and learning. During our journey, we discovered certain "keys" that are enabling us to have a wonderful and fabulous marriage relationship, one that grows richer and more exciting every day.

We have great news to share: The great news is that these keys are available to every couple reading this book. With the help of these keys, you too will be enjoying your very own special version of the most wonderful marriage on planet earth!

We believe with every fiber of our being that if we could place a dose of what we have learned into each and every marriage in America and elsewhere, every relationship would be dramatically improved and the world would be the better for it.

"If Joel and Kathy can do it, so can you!"

Yes, there **is** hope for **you!**

In the earliest days of our marriage we kept in mind that having a successful marriage did not depend on finding the right person. Having a successful marriage depended on being the right person. Little did we realize where our journey of becoming the right persons would take us!

Calling All Men!

Regardless of whether your character flaws lie in the areas of abuse, adultery, workaholic tendencies or substance abuse there is hope for you. If your challenge is that you simply cannot figure out how to improve your marriage relationship, there is hope for you, too!

You can overcome your issues. You can become the man that God has called you to become.

The answer to every issue a man may have lies in the answer to one question.

The **answer to adultery** lies in the answer to one question.

The **answer to an abusive relationship** lies in the answer to one question.

The **answer to how you can have an absolutely fabulous marriage** to the wife of your youth lies in the answer to one question.

The key that will enable your wife to **become the most fabulous wife who fulfills your hopes and dreams** lies in the answer to one question.

GOLDEN KEY

HOW DO I BECOME THE MAN THAT GOD HAS CALLED ME TO BE?

Dear Joel and Kathy,

We were blessed to meet you in Houston, Texas, at the Charles & Frances Hunter Healing Explosion. I was given a wonderful opportunity to sing in the Friday morning session. My husband and I read your book. We bought several and sowed them into others' lives in and out of our ministry here in Shreveport.

When I read the book I was amazed at how it seemed to reach inside of me and began to change me as I read. It truly is the secret to having the most successful marriage anyone ever imagined. Most powerful! I read certain chapters twice and will read all of it again.

Ever since we read the book, I've seen how differently we have dealt with daily issues when they come up. It's like having the opportunity to be newlywed all over again and grow up the right way in marriage! Smile. We laugh a lot more than we used to, a noticeable difference. The Holy Spirit truly brings comfort and guidance when "letting" HIM do the work through our willingness to change.

My husband, Pastor Lance Alexander, promoted the book by lighting a flame into the hearts and minds of couples simply by telling everyone the TRUTH about the book. He said, "This book will ultimately change the way you see yourself first, then each other, and your marriage will never be the same after you read it." We came back from Houston excited and ready to start passing the books out. My marriage, my life will never be the same.

God bless you for obeying the voice of the Lord and sowing much time and effort into writing such a life-changing book.

Vernell Alexander,
Rivers of Life Christian Ministries, Shreveport, Louisiana

Chapter Two

The Dream

Where there is **no vision** *the people perish.*
Proverbs 29:18

Whatsoever things **you desire** *when* **you pray,**
believe that you receive them and **you shall have**
them.
Mark 11:24

By Kathy

I have been asked many times what kept me in the marriage with Joel during those first 10 hard years.

All things considered, I did the only thing I could. I clung to and relied upon the Word of God.

The Word declares that you must have a vision for your marriage or it will perish. In my heart of hearts, I have always known that without a vision our marriage would have perished – and I have acted accordingly.

When Joel and I married, we had a powerful vision of our lives together. Among other things, we had received a prophetic word concerning our future marriage and ministry as a couple. Together, we would touch the world!

The word we received was, "You will be married and I will touch many through you as a couple."

I also had the vision of having a perfect dream marriage. I did not want to give up on our future, regardless of what it took!

At one time every woman had a dream. It might be a dim memory today but it was once crystal clear. Take it from me, that dream can become a reality.

What is the dream? It is the one you had as a little girl: the dream that one day you would marry a man, who would treat you first like a princess – and then like a queen.

Your thoughts and feelings, your desires and cares would be as important and as valuable to this man as they would be to you.

> **YOU AND THE THINGS YOU HAD TO SAY WOULD BE VERY IMPORTANT AND VALUABLE TO THIS MAN.**

Maybe those exact words did not cross your mind as a little girl but the dream of the **wonderful way** you would be treated by your future husband, the man of your dreams, certainly did.

You watched "Cinderella" and, even though you knew it was a fairy tale, you were sure the man you would marry would be equivalent to any fairy tale prince.

Unbelievably, your husband actually had a dream of being a prince to his princess!

He really thought that he could get married and automatically be the perfect husband for the perfect wife!

Tragically, this dream goes by the wayside for most men in about three days after the wedding when they realize this marriage relationship is going to take work to enjoy!

You grew up, fell in love and got married. In a few days, months or years the **reality of your** married life hit and you became painfully aware that the reality you were experiencing did not match your cherished dream!

All of a sudden your prince, your "knight in shining armor" turned out to be a control freak wanting everything his way or no way.

He began expecting or possibly even demanding that you take care of **everything** at home: the children, the house, the cooking and the cleaning – while his sole duty was to go to work. Moreover, if you worked outside the home you discovered that he expected you to do all of this in **addition** to your job!

Your picture of his arriving home and the two of you enjoying the rest of the evening was replaced by a reality of his not wanting to do anything to be a blessing to you.

The idea was that his workday was done and it was time for him to be served while you continued your 18-hour day of childcare, cook, housekeeper and sex goddess!

Your dream of him opening doors for you is gone. The dream of him asking, "What can I do to help you?" "What would you like to do tonight?" or "What movie would you like to watch?" vanishes. Instead you hear, "Where's the TV remote control?"

There it is! That word *Control!*

"Me Tarzan – You Jane! Me boss – You slave!"

Does this sound familiar? Perhaps your marital experience looks in some small way like the marriage of Scott and Tamara. Scott is a well-known "Man of God" in the community and in the church. He is in charge of a regional ministry and regularly wins a "Lay Minister of the Year" award. Scott looks like the ideal husband.

Incidentally, many manipulative and controlling men have this appearance to anyone looking on from the outside.

Scott demanded that Tamara home school their daughter. Tamara enjoyed home schooling when she first started. It grew tiring and she decided to enroll her daughter back into a traditional school. Scott informed Tamara that if she quit home schooling that he would divorce her, take their daughter and leave her with nothing.

This does not seem possible. How could he control her with this threat? Here's how:

Scott has manipulated their financial life so that everything is in his name only: the house, the cars, and the bank accounts. Scott gives Tamara money with which she is required to pay the household bills, buy food, gasoline and pay for any additional expenses that appear. On paper they are millionaires, but Tamara has to pinch pennies because the amount she is rationed does not cover the bills. Scott comes home and does nothing but bury himself in the newspaper. If Tamara does not keep the house spotless she is sternly taken to task.

Moreover, Scott and Tamara do not have a sex life. Why? Tamara is concerned about the reliability of birth control methods. I can appreciate her concern; because Joel and I conceived at least one child while using each popular form of birth control.

Tamara's last pregnancy resulted in a miscarriage. Had the child been carried to full term there would have been severe complications. Because of this concern, Tamara is willing to have a tubal ligation but Scott refuses to pay for the surgery, a $4,000 procedure. Why doesn't Scott get a low cost vasectomy to fix the problem? He just does not want to. End result? No sex.

In our last contact with them, Tamara was afraid to ask their Pastor for help. She believed there was no hope that the Pastor would believe her or be able to help her. Scott is too sharp. Like most manipulative and controlling Christian husbands, he can turn anything she says around and make her look like the "bad guy". Tamara is convinced that any attempt to expose Scott will totally backfire.

Ladies, you might not be experiencing a nightmare marriage to the degree that Tamara is. You might not be experiencing emotional, spiritual and mental abuses to the degree that I experienced with Joel – but you are suffering. Your pain is **yours** and **yours alone** – it is **now** – and it is **real.** Your **disappointment** is yours and yours alone. This is what counts today.

What happened to the dream of your husband doing the dishes or having the children to help? Where is that dream of the two of you taking a walk, hand in hand, on the beach? Do you walk *anywhere* hand in hand?

> **YOUR PAIN IS YOURS — IT IS NOW — AND IT IS REAL. YOUR DISAPPOINTMENT IS YOURS AND YOURS ALONE. THIS IS WHAT COUNTS TODAY.**

What happened to the dream of the two of you having a nice quiet dinner out while the children are with a sitter?

Can you remember the dream in which the things that you had to say would be important to him and he would let you know in so many ways how important, valuable and needed you were?

You had a dream of what married life could be like. Your dream stands in stark contrast to the current idea of marriage which is simply two people sharing the same house and each paying half of the bills.

The sad truth is that after just a few short months

or years, many marriages become merely convenient "living arrangements" that lack fun, passion, sensitivity and excitement.

Our message to both of you is that there is hope! Your dream **can** be a reality! Dreams do come true! The honeymoon does not have to end. You **can** have a honeymoon that lasts an entire lifetime!

Joel and I laughed recently when we read a line in a book on romance. The author was described as "still a newlywed, after **three** years." Three years? I hope he has a long and happy marriage, but at three years a marriage has only just begun!

Joel and I have been married over 22 years. Ten of those years at times seemed like a living hell.

We pastored a church in the late eighties and survived an adultery experience, which is one of the worst attacks a marriage can go through. We elaborate on this and some other hard experiences that we have had throughout the remainder of this book.

What is important now is that we have come through to the other side. People comment to us regularly that we must either be newlyweds or on our honeymoon. I am living my dream-come-true marriage. We are more in love today than ever.

I am married to the man of my dreams and he tells me that he is married to the woman of his. If we can come through the rough waters we have come through then I can assure you that you can come through yours!

"If Joel and Kathy can do it, You can do it too!"

You **can** have a dream-come-true marriage. It does not matter if you currently have an average marriage or an above average marriage. It does not matter if you have a bad marriage or a marriage that is on the rocks.

You can see improvement in your marriage. Your marriage can be restored or even resurrected from the dead!

How can this happen? That is what this book is all about. Your husband can make your dreams come true and you can make his dreams come true.

> **Grace to you and peace** *from our Father and the Lord Jesus Christ.*
> *Ephesians 1:1*

For you to do your part in your marriage you are going to need God's grace.

God's grace is His ability and strength made available to you.

God's grace will empower you to make it beyond **just living** to where you find yourself living your **dream** marriage. God's grace will bring you into the place of inner peace that comes when you know that God is working on your behalf when your relationship is facing challenges.

The grace and peace of God speak. They assure you that the dream that you had growing up is a God-given dream that He still wants to bring to pass.

In Him

The book of Ephesians speaks often of being "in Him." My question to you is "Are you in Him?"

> **WITHOUT A RELATIONSHIP WITH JESUS AND THE HOLY SPIRIT, YOU WILL BE LIVING IN YOUR OWN STRENGTH AND THAT CAN BE VERY TIRING.**

Until you establish a personal relationship with Jesus and the Holy Spirit, you will be living in your own strength. Talk about tiring!

If it weren't for my relationship with the Holy Spirit, I would have never been able to accomplish the things that have contributed to our happy marriage.

On April 1, 1991, when I learned of Joel's adultery, the stress and feelings of betrayal were so overwhelming that I checked myself into a hospital. It "floored" me to realize that the things I had suspected were actually true concerning Joel and the other woman, who had been my close friend.

21

I had chosen to believe that Joel could not be having an affair. I had chosen to believe the logical denials he would offer when I voiced my concerns. I had chosen to *believe the best* about Joel in accordance with 1 Corinthians 13 – the Love Chapter of the Bible.

After all, Joel was the pastor. He was "on fire" for Jesus. Miracles were occurring in our church on a regular basis. Joel couldn't be having an affair. He certainly would not be **lying** about it.

Sure we'd had some disappointments when church members let us down. Sure we'd had some setbacks as everyone in ministry has had at times. But adultery was **not** the outcome I expected from all of our dedication and hard labor. This was unbelievable.

When I realized that all of my faith and confidence in Joel was for naught, I was devastated – to put it mildly.

Thank God, I did not let the very normal reluctance to seek help stop me from checking myself into the hospital. In the midst of my utter confusion and overwhelming despair, somehow, the Holy Spirit led me to seek this immediate, temporary assistance.

I remember waiting in the emergency room to talk with a doctor about being admitted. A curious nurse came by and asked what was going on. My mother-in-law and friends explained to her that the pastor of the church ran off with another woman from the congregation and that his wife was distraught and in need of help.

The nurse still did not "get the drift." She looked at me and asked, "Well, who are you?" With buckets of tears streaming down my face and looking like a sad puppy, I cried out, "I'm the pastor's wiiiiiiiffffffe...." It was a pathetic moment. Oh, it is funny **now**. But on that fateful day, it was just pathetic.

I don't remember what happened next except that "they" were all talking about how long I should be "committed". I insisted that I was only checking in for three days. With this stipulation, I signed the papers to be admitted.

Only God knows what may have happened if I had tried to cope with this shock to my emotional system on my own. Thank God, I knew there is no shame in seeking professional help if you need it. Getting help is far better than committing murder or suicide!

Upon admission to the hospital, I was given an anti-depressant. It cleared my mind, which enabled me to focus on God and pray for direction as to what to do next concerning this horrible "situation". I knew that I had to rest and prepare myself to care for our two children when I got out. I had three days to get myself together. I called my parents, I called friends, I called pastors, and I called anyone who I thought could help me. As the hours progressed, my thinking became progressively clearer.

I knew what I had to do – as hard as it was. I made a quality decision to forgive and forge ahead. I wrote Joel a letter that very night, a letter flowing with forgiveness, a letter letting him know that God and I had not given up on God's dream for us. I chose to believe that God could restore us! That was God's grace and peace working through me. My confidence in God assured me that if I bought some time, God would work on Joel and once again capture his heart.

This same confidence in God and His wonder-working power, which I had seen demonstrated many times in my own life, gave me the strength, commitment, and patience to begin the necessary work on my marriage. Necessary work. There are no other words to describe it: I worked and I worked hard. I prayed and I prayed hard. I stood on God's promises. And I stood, even when it seemed hopeless. All the work paid off. Today, I enjoy the fruits of my labors every day and it is a wonderful life. What I believed, I received! God did indeed work on Joel and dramatically captured and changed his heart.

For the first ten years of my marriage, I stood, but change did not result. The change resulted when Joel was finally confronted by truth. Your days of "standing" are coming to a close. The truth in this book is your fork in the road; as it was for us. You are going to discover new ways of looking at marriage that will set you free. Your patience will now be coupled with knowledge that works! The truth will set you free, and the truth will set your husband free!

How did I do this?

Ladies, in the portions of the book I have written, I am going to share with you what I did to keep peace in our home until this knowledge came. I am going to let you in on what was my part in keeping Joel and me together long enough to give God time to work on my behalf. In the process I will share practical things that you can do to improve your marriage relationship starting **right now**.

In addition, Joel and I will stand on your husband's toes. We will require him to grow up and quit resisting your desire that he be the man of your dreams! And when you respond positively to his efforts it will make his transformation from "selfish heel" to the "man of your dreams" a little easier and a little quicker! This transformation will not only benefit the two of you, it will benefit any children you may have. They will learn from your example that married life can be peaceful, happy, safe and secure – and very, very exciting!

Here is a verse that became very important to me. I trusted that God would not forget the labor of love that I showed toward him by ministering to Joel. Make this verse very important to you:

> *"For God is not unjust to forget your work and labor of love that you have shown toward His name, in that you have ministered to the saints."*
> *Hebrews 6:10*

GOLDEN KEY

IF YOU BELIEVE IN YOUR DREAM YOU CAN LIVE THAT DREAM

Joel and Kathy,

We met at the National Christian Counselors Association meeting in Orlando.

I want you to know your book is changing lives!

My husband has changed his attitude and is treating me like I'm his bride. We've been married 15 years. I hooked him on the book by reading him chapter 20 first! Hee hee hee!

One of my brothers is reading it and can't put it down. After 20 years of marriage, his wife says he is now making changes and is even getting up in the middle of the night to read it. He is going to buy one of your books and give it to my other brother for his birthday.

I am getting such wonderful results with "The Man of Her Dreams/The Woman of His!" in my counseling practice. I work for a secular organization and one of the therapists has ordered four copies from me! He says he is going to give them to his daughters. I am so excited!

I plan to make the books available to our church near Valentine's Day. I know I will get a great response from our congregation.

I'll be in touch,
Allyssa Monroe, Alabama

<u>Authors' Note</u>
As soon as marriage counselors see the change that comes when they "prescribe" this book to their clients, it becomes an indispensable tool to bring lasting change to those who seek their guidance. Each reader can help by introducing a professional Christian marriage counselor to "The Man of Her Dreams/The Woman of His!" in your area.

Chapter Three

This Woman You Gave Me, Lord!

*But **it was the woman you gave me** who brought me the fruit and I ate it.*

Genesis 3:12 (NLB)

By Joel

When our marriage was going through its worst times I was a master at manipulating Kathy. I did it in a manner that would enable me to convince anyone in our world that Kathy was at fault for any problem we had.

Boiled down to the bottom line, the problems all worked like this: Kathy would express a need. I was childish and therefore the need would touch my insecurities and overwhelm me. I could not bring myself to simply meet her need.

I despised any signs of weakness in Kathy. Instead of embracing her when she would express a need, I would be repelled. I would recoil in anger at her attempts to touch a place of tenderness in me. My insecurities stopped me from welcoming her into my heart and propelled me away from lovingly meeting her need. Understand that I was often tender but it was always on my terms and in my timing, yet when Kathy needed and requested tenderness from me, it was not available.

Instead the walls would go up and I would say something to put her off. "You don't need a hug right now." "You don't need to talk to me. You need to talk to God." "I did not look at you in a condescending way."

From here things would escalate to the point where Kathy would scream or throw a plate at me! Now I had my ammo! I had all the proof that I needed to justify **that I was the good guy.** Kathy was unstable!

One especially frustrating time for Kathy was when I arrived home after working on the road for four days. Kathy had worked continuously taking care of our three children and preparing our home so it would be just right when I returned.

Our third child, Josiah, was a newborn and he had jaundice. Kathy had to keep him on the windowsill in the sun or under a "plant-grow" light. Chris and Jen were very active five- and four- year- olds, respectively. Needless to say, Kathy was always on the edge of exhaustion or a nervous breakdown. To make matters worse she felt like she had to keep everything perfect in our world so that I would not put her down.

When I pulled up to the house I realized that Kathy had parked four feet over into my parking place and I could not fit my car in. I got out, moved her vehicle and went into the house in a huff. Instead of greeting her and the children with a loving kiss and embrace, I rudely informed her that she had parked exactly how I had specifically told her not to park the week before!

Rather than noticing how clean and organized the house was, a window blind caught my eye. "Kathy, didn't I tell you I like to keep the blinds up to let the light in?"

This was one of those times where my mental and emotional abuse was just too much. Kathy escalated and I escalated further. She pulled a friend out of a church service and proceeded to express her frustrations telling her that God had to do something quick because she could not handle this anymore.

It was not long after this that one of our arguments grew to the point that Kathy hit me in the chest. Being bigger, stronger and always needing to reinforce that I was in control, I grabbed her and wrestled her to the ground. I hit her on the back once to get my point across that "I indeed am bigger and stronger. You had better not take a swing at me." The hit on her back did not hurt or leave a bruise or mark. I was determined to put Kathy in her place by utilizing physical restraint and mental, emotional, or spiritual abuse.

> I HAD YEARS OF EVIDENCE OF KATHY CAUSING PROBLEMS IN OUR MARRIAGE.

Kathy called a mutual friend; her husband came over to confront me. He said, "Joel, did you hit your wife?" I insisted that I had simply been protecting myself. He walked out, bewildered and not knowing how to answer my defense. He simply said, as he left, "Joel, you can't hit your wife."

In my mind, I had been totally justified in this "physical restraint." In retrospect, it had not hurt when Kathy hit me in the chest. I was in no danger. This incident was only a continuation in my game of one-upmanship.

This type of physical altercation happened perhaps four times in those difficult first ten years. (1984-1994). The bottom line in my mind was that **Kathy** was at fault for every one of these "restraining encounters" as well as every other problem in our marriage! I was simply a victim who was "protecting" myself. My insecurities hindered me from simply meeting Kathy's needs. Instead, I was willing to get into yelling and screaming matches, which occasionally climaxed in these physical situations.

As long as I could push Kathy to act in a way that I could point to as proof that she was at fault, I was satisfied. My ego and pride were intact and justified. Totally ridiculous, isn't it? Yet these same patterns are repeated in hundreds of thousands of Christian homes every day. Some are to the same degree, some are not as bad and some are worse.

When we landed in Colorado for the Life Skills Ministry seminar on marriage counseling I had years of evidence of Kathy causing problems in our marriage.

I had been successful at convincing everyone in our world that Kathy was the source of the trouble in our marriage. When Kathy would reach out to a pastor or anyone else who might help, I could easily convince the person that Kathy was to blame. If I had read this paragraph at the time, my response would have been, "Well, that is just great for you, but in my marriage, Kathy really is the one at fault." Not only would I have said this, I would have firmly believed it. Compounding our problems was that Kathy had been "duped" by wrong teaching in the church; teaching that told her that God could "fix" our marriage if she would only submit, respect me and pray more. This is a recipe for failure in a troubled Christian marriage. Is there any wonder that we have a 50% divorce rate in the Body of Christ?

We sat for the first few hours as the founder of Life Skills International, Paul Hegstrom, emphasized the role of men in a relationship and **their responsibilities** to their wives. Finally, I could stand it no more. I publicly asked Paul, "Okay, so we have been talking to men for a few hours now. When do we talk about what the women have to do?"

> **CAN'T THE WOMAN BE THE PROBLEM? THE MAN IS NOT ALWAYS THE PROBLEM IN MARRIAGE.**

To this he replied, "When a man gets his issues straight and meets his wife's needs, most of her issues will go away and she will begin to respond in a positive way." I **did not** like that answer! That answer insinuated that our problems might partially be my fault when clearly they were all Kathy's fault! I just knew that I could convince Paul of this fact if given the chance, so I waited for my opportunity.

A few more hours into the training, I repeated the question in another manner. "Can't the **woman** be the problem? The man is not **always** the problem in marriage." Of course I gestured toward **my problem wife!** This continued into the second day until Dr. Hegstrom finally had enough. He told me point blank that **I** was the problem in my marriage. He told me that Kathy was desperate to have a great marriage relationship for that is how God made her.

He continued, saying that my issues had caused the problems in our marriage and that if I would get healed and change that I would have a most incredible wife. He emphatically stated that she might have some very minor issues that need to be addressed but that she will deal with those on her own **after** I have dealt with mine.

Paul told me that God made Kathy a responder and that her problems were a reflection of her responding to my treatment of her. He said that when I grow up and lay my life down for my wife as Christ did for the church that I would be amazed at how wonderful a wife I have.

This was the beginning. A seed was planted. I did not change overnight but my perception gradually began to change. I began to realize that I had been at fault in our problems. I began to see that my pride, insecurity and immaturity caused me to run from Kathy's needs instead of reaching out to meet them.

I began to see why I required that everything originate with me. My ways of expressing my love for Kathy always had to be my idea. If I suggested we go out to dinner or if I bought her flowers then I was happy to express love to her. However, when it was her idea (or demand, as I saw it) I would throw down the gauntlet. I would tell her that she was too needy.

As far as I was concerned, any needs that she expressed were illegitimate and were signs of weakness. I was unwilling to attempt meeting her needs. In my opinion they were too deep. I would rudely instruct Kathy to talk to the Lord by declaring, "I can't help you! You are a bottomless pit of needs. Talk to God or a girlfriend. Just leave **me** alone!"

I could not admit when I did something wrong. My insecurities were too deep, my pride insurmountable. I felt like I would lose something if I admitted that I had made a mistake. As God began to let me see our marital problems in the light of truth it all began to dawn on me. I had been the problem all along! If only I had been dead to myself while being willing to meet my wife's needs, we would not have had 99% of our problems.

> **IF I HAD MUTUALLY SUBMITTED TO HER INSTEAD OF DEMANDING THAT SHE SUBMIT TO ME, WE WOULD HAVE BEEN SAVED FROM YEARS OF GRIEF.**

If I had **mutually submitted** to her instead of demanding that she submit to me, we would have been saved from years of grief. I would like to tell you that our marriage miraculously turned around in 24 hours after the seminar that we attended. The truth is that it took a couple years for the seeds that were planted on that weekend to come to fruition in a way that made enough of a meaningful difference in our lives that Kathy could relax.

Kathy was very excited after the seminar and could see immediately that seeds of change were planted in me. The following six months were especially difficult for Kathy because she knew that I had received the knowledge but I continued to struggle with the paradigm shift regularly. A number of times Kathy grew so frustrated that she would call Paul Hegstrom's office in Colorado to receive counsel from him.

In one of these conversations Paul told Kathy that she should start setting money aside in order to fund a temporary separation. He felt that this would cause the changes to happen more quickly. Kathy decided against this plan of action but I mention it to present the reality of our situation and to bring a hopeful message that your marriage can be healed regardless of the severity of your difficulties.

The job that I had at the time took me away from home four days a week. I would be on the road three times per month leaving Monday night and returning on Friday. At times Kathy would be ready for me to hit the road again on Saturday!

We worked at improving our relationship, though. I asked Kathy to confront me when I was being verbally, emotionally or spiritually abusive. I asked her to remind me of the things that we learned and hold me accountable.

I needed to treat her in a way that acknowledged her value.

Kathy was patient. I could get away with a little bit of insensitivity, put-downs or bad treatment of her. We made an agreement to use a signal so that I could begin to identify when my attitudes were unacceptable.

If I were in a bad mood she would try to gently soothe me by offering me a quiet place to relax with a cup of tea or suggesting that I go out to a movie. When this did not help and I would continue pushing on her she would get her fill and use the pre-chosen and agreed upon words, "jerk" or "heel." At this signal I would immediately drop the subject and back off.

I still remember pushing on Kathy emotionally and her saying things like, "If you don't quit, God will not answer your prayers!" Sometimes she would demand to know if I was going to live the Word or just teach it!

Many times Kathy would tell me that I was being manipulative and controlling. I would disagree and we would proceed to argue over whether or not I was being manipulative and controlling! A few days later I would admit to her and myself that yes, I indeed had been acting abusively **again!**

My growing up and meeting Kathy's needs was a very difficult process. Paul Hegstrom and a lady pastor that Kathy would confide in both told her that the time would have been shortened had she separated from me. It was a personal decision that Kathy made not to leave. We never tell women that they are required to stay in an abusive situation regardless of whether the abuse is physical, mental, emotional or spiritual.

Kathy has always been dedicated and committed to our having a successful marriage. She looked for every positive sign that I was making progress and that there was hope for our relationship.

I almost broke this mechanism in her, but by the grace of God, Kathy stuck with it. In the recovery years after Life Skills, she was not just blindly "standing" with no relief in sight. Kathy was holding me accountable to change using what we learned and had the "right" to speak up regularly in defense of herself. It was my job to acknowledge her concerns and change.

> **MEN, HERE IT IS. YOUR WIFE WANTS A FABULOUS RELATIONSHIP WITH YOU. GOD MADE HER THAT WAY.**

Today, she brags about me everywhere she goes and we enjoy a wonderful relationship. I am the man of her dreams and she truly is the woman of mine. Men, here it is. Your wife wants a fabulous and happy relationship with you. God made her that way. In Genesis God spoke to your wife concerning this desire that she would have **for you**.

Your desire shall be for your husband.
Genesis 3:16

She wants you, baby, she wants you! However, **what God created your wife to desire is a deep, meaningful, bonded, successful relationship with you.**

Bonding with your wife is a difficult thing to describe. Bonding is believing that you are equals. Bonding is treating each other with love and respect. Bonding is loving the thoughts of your partner.

Bonding is being sensitive to not hurt the one you love. Bonding is becoming 'one flesh.' Bonding is two hearts beating as one. When you are bonded you are not manipulating and controlling your wife. You are not demanding that she serve you. You truly love her for who she is. When you are bonded to your wife she always knows where you are and what you are doing. You are never doing your own thing in order to maintain your independence.

At the same time you are not demanding that your wife be under your thumb. You are encouraging her independence and growth. You **want** her to be confident. You **want** her to know that if something were ever to happen to you that she would be perfectly capable of living a successful life.

Everything in your wife is designed by God to work toward a bonded relationship with her husband. If you will simply grow up, meet her needs, die to yourself and give your life for your mate, then her "ticker" will work automatically. In short order you will discover that you have a most incredible wife!

37

God made this real easy for us men, if we will simply lay down our lives for our wives and meet their needs. When you quit throwing mud into your wife's heart, she will respond to you with love, affection, respect and everything else that you are trying to force her to do.

The key to this is that you become the man that God has called you to be by becoming the husband that your wife needs you to be.

It was difficult for me to bring down the walls of "self protection" in my heart when Kathy expressed a need to bond with me. It was not just difficult. It was almost impossible. I could not stand the negative feelings that were generated in me when she would ask me to "listen to her heart" or "listen to her feelings." She was hurting and I was the cause. I did not want to hear that!

I protected myself from bonding with Kathy by "throwing down the gauntlet" regularly. If we were discussing something and I wanted to quit talking about it I would tell Kathy that the subject was closed. She would try to get me to talk it out in order to get that all-important sense of closure. I would tell her that she was being rebellious and unsubmissive. "I said that the conversation is over and so it is over! I am the head of this house and it is sin for you to demand that we talk further about it. You have to repent and get your heart right."

A horrible example was when I came back from the adultery. I demanded, "The adultery is over. I have repented and you can never mention it again." I was too insecure to handle the "feeling" of her pain.

For three years I could not bring myself to embrace the depths of hurt that my action had caused. I did not want to "go there." Adultery hurts a wife worse emotionally than any other thing that a husband can do. A husband who does this is the "lowest of the low." It is amazing that these same husbands still see themselves as "God's gift to women!"

Male adulterers are almost incorrigible flirters! Kathy had to point out to me repeatedly for a couple of years when I was flirting so that I could recognize and stop it! The first few times Kathy said that I was flirting I resisted her but then I started to recognize the pattern. Listen to your wife, men. God gave her to you to help you grow up and become the man that He has called you to become!

> **THE ONLY WAY THAT YOU WILL BECOME THE MAN THAT GOD HAS CALLED YOU TO BE IS BY BECOMING THE HUSBAND THAT YOUR WIFE NEEDS YOU TO BE.**

I put a lot of effort toward loving Kathy in those first ten years of marriage. It was on my terms, of course. I would pour out tokens of love on her, we had regular "date nights" like all of the marriage books suggest and I made sure that all of the special occasions were celebrated.

Remember that we were in public ministry the entire first ten years of our marriage when all of this was going on. We wanted to have a great marriage and we truly worked hard at it. The problem was that we were trying everything according to my terms; after all, I was the head of the house and Kathy had to follow.

Listen, guys, your wife is a gift given to you from God for a purpose. God gave your wife to you so that you could become the man that He has called you to be.

The only way that you will become the man that God has called **you to be** is by becoming the husband that your wife **needs you to be**.

In order to meet your wife's individual and particular needs you may have to grow up and mature.

When you are successfully meeting her needs and she is a happy wife, you can be certain that you are growing into the man that God has called you to become.

GOLDEN KEY

YOUR WIFE WANTS A DEEP, MEANINGFUL, BONDED, SUCCESSFUL RELATIONSHIP WITH YOU!

Dear Joel and Kathy,

This book has changed my life! Before reading it I felt like my 12-year marriage to Christine was at a dead end; there was no place to turn for help.

I believed that Christine was to blame for all of our marital problems. I would often remind her of her faults. I felt that that Christine was always nagging and complaining. No matter how many times I tried to correct her of this, it only made the situation worse. Christine would mention divorce on a regular basis, saying that she wished she had never married me. She would often lose her temper and would sometimes throw things at me in disgust. Our situation appeared hopeless.

I had done everything I knew to change Christine! I would pray for hours at a time and wonder why God would never change her! Nothing that I said or did made a difference. I could argue for hours as to why I was such a good husband and was not to blame for any of our problems. I left the marriage for another woman. Christine and I each had an attorney in whom we trusted to take care of the details. That would be the end of it (or so we thought).

Praise God! Divorce was not God's plan for our lives! I thank God for "The Man of Her Dreams/The Woman of His!" Without it I would have missed out on the best years of my life and caused much harm to Christine and our children. How could I ever have been so deceived?

Christine read "The Man of Her Dreams/The Woman of His!" first. When she told me how much the book meant to her I insisted that it must be one-sided. If Christine agreed with it then it must be wrong! Christine told me that it spoke to both men and women and I wanted to find the things that spoke to the women! I began to read the book!

After reading the first few chapters I was irate. I looked forward to calling the authors in the morning to tell them how wrong they were about marriage relationships! I was not to blame! Christine was the problem! As I continued reading, the Holy Spirit moved in my heart and the scales fell from my eyes. I began to see that Christine was the woman of my dreams! Ninety pages later I fully realized that Joel and Kathy Davisson couldn't have been more correct regarding husbands and wives.

"The Man of Her Dreams/The Woman of His!" began to change my life. I could hardly believe that I had been blind to so many things that were now crystal clear concerning the problems in our marriage. I confessed to Christine that it was I who had been wrong all along. Before those scales were removed I truly had no idea that it was I who had the problems! I had been sincere but wrong!

As I applied the principles in Joel and Kathy's book, our relationship immediately changed for the better. I have gotten my act together; Christine's problems have magically disappeared! I never would have believed this to be possible until I experienced it myself.

Christine and I feel like young teenagers in love again! Every aspect of our life is full of hope and excitement! I praise God for the forgiveness and patience that Christine has extended to me and for the life that we now have together.

Thank you from the bottom of my heart, Joel and Kathy, for showing me how to be "The Man of Her Dreams". Christine surely is "The Woman of Mine!" If not for your book I would have missed out on all of the beautiful years that God has in store for my future as a husband to Christine. My three precious children would have missed out on having me as resident "daddy" and I would have missed out on being resident "daddy" to them. How blessed we as a family are.

May God bless you both,
Kenneth Robinson, Tulsa, Oklahoma

<u>Authors' Note</u>
To learn more about this couple and how their lives have been changed, read the testimony from Christine Robinson at the end of the Chapter 4.

Something to Think About

NOT AS BAD AS OURS
By Joel

Your marriage may not be as bad as ours was. That is irrelevant. The Bible says that if you compare yourself among yourselves that you are unwise.

You may have never committed adultery. That is irrelevant. Jesus said that if you look on a woman to lust, you have already committed adultery with her in your heart.

It does not matter if your marriage is better or if it is worse than ours was. The principles that God taught us will work for every marriage.

When we went to Colorado, I realized immediately that Paul Hegstrom's marriage had been worse than ours. Paul would physically beat his wife, Judy, and leave her bloody and bruised. He had more than one affair. Paul divorced Judy and was arrested for attempted murder when he threw his live-in girlfriend down a flight of steps, almost killing her. Judy and Paul later remarried. I also noted that Paul and I had different personalities and that Kathy and Judy had different personalities.

But I listened. I learned. Truth be told, Paul had to pry my brain open with a crowbar and force me to listen instead of just hearing, but I accepted the message.

I was not as bad a husband as Paul had been. But, unlike others, I did not hide behind this convenient excuse to not deal with my issues. I saw the patterns in myself. I saw the tendencies to avoid meeting Kathy's needs. Paul's story had some similarities to mine - and some differences - but the heart issues were almost identical. The heart issues are universal.

We started this book with the adultery expose' for a number of reasons. First, it happened. It is a part of our history. If our transparency will help others recover from marital failures, then we are glad to be of assistance by being transparent. Secondly, we wanted to get your attention. Many men are fascinated by the fact that pastors are falling into adultery. Our story gives some insight into this horrendous epidemic.

The fact is, though, that the adultery was a very small window in our marriage. We had serious issues for seven years before and three years after the adultery. These other issues and our healing in these other areas are much more important to the success of this book in helping your marriage than the adultery. Even if you have committed adultery, that fact contributes to only about five percent of the problems that are present in your marriage. I do not minimize that. There are indeed serious trust issues that have to be dealt with now in the aftermath and much healing is needed. The principles that you learn in this book will naturally guide you successfully through this particular landmine in the course of dealing with the underlying marriage issues that plague most Christian marriages, not only yours.

All of these other issues are what we aim to successfully deal with. Don't get sidetracked about the adultery issue. That is just a symptom that may or may not be present in your own marriage. If adultery is not one of your symptoms, try these on for size: Loud arguments, constant misunderstandings, put-downs, power struggles, lack of sexual fulfillment, disagreements over how to raise kids, money arguments, someone watches TV constantly, hurt feelings, residual hurts from childhood that cause major contentions today and severe marital difficulties in second and third marriages.

This book has the answer to all of these difficulties and every other difficulty that plagues Christian marriages. If you will allow the Holy Spirit to change you as you prayerfully read the rest of this book, He will customize the principles to your individual marriage problems.

Welcome to a new world. If you will seriously and prayerfully read this whole book with a teachable spirit, your life will never be the same.

As Frances Hunter proclaims, this book puts into a nutshell the answer to every problem in every marriage. You can implement the answers on your own and receive your miracle without ever speaking to us as so many other "now happily married" couples have done. However, if you both have read the complete book, if you have talked it over and the Holy Spirit has not shown you how to apply the principles to your particular situation, and if you both are serious about restoration, you may call us for personal counseling. We won't charge a set fee, but if we help you find your way to your miracle, we will accept a gift of appreciation for the time that we spend with you.

Chapter Four

Did I Ever Feel
Like Quitting?

God is not unjust to **forget your work and**
labor of love, which *you have shown toward*
his name in that **you have ministered to his**
servants.

Hebrews 6:10 (condensed)

By Kathy

The Holy Spirit spoke to Joel telling him that we
would be married and that He would touch many people
through us as a couple. I was excited to get onto this God-
inspired train! Joel loved the Lord and was called into
ministry. I loved the Lord and wanted to work with him.
Life would be easy! Joel and I would serve the Lord
together, have children and live happily ever after!

There was a small warning and harbinger of things
to come. On the day before Joel and I got married, I asked
him to help me get the suitcases packed for our
honeymoon. (Yes, we waited until our honeymoon to
consummate our marriage.)

Joel informed me that it was my job to pack
suitcases. He said that his mom packed for his family and
he expected me to do the same. I commented that my
mother also packed often for my dad when they went
away and I did my assigned task with a smile.

The red flags were waving and I entertained 20 minutes of doubt. We went ahead and got married. After all, I was getting married and my husband to be had shown me all of the wonderful books on marriage that he had read. Ours would be a wonderful relationship filled with joy, peace, the Holy Spirit, ministry and Jesus!

I soon realized that instead of a nice relaxing ride on rails through the countryside, our marriage was more like a rollercoaster! I found the perfect coaster to describe our life when we visited "Islands of Adventure" in Orlando, Florida. It was "The Hulk."

"The Hulk" catapults you into the unknown, where you experience high speeds, sudden turns and you are even riding upside down two or three times!

Our marriage was always quite an up and down event. We had fun times punctuated by screaming sessions. There were exciting ministry adventures accompanied by the revelation that Joel was a master of manipulation and control. We enjoyed a variety of travel while I endured the stings of Joel's public put-downs.

Our first two children were born in the midst of many financial challenges. Our later business interests, which included traveling as a family, enabled us to eat in many fine restaurants while our problems would get us thinking that we would never make it.

We always have enjoyed plenty of lovemaking while at the same time Joel would not be sensitive to my thoughts and feelings.

I tried everything that I could to make our marriage a success including reading many books on submission and practicing what they taught. I dedicated myself to making sure that everything was done Joel's way. I would leave love notes and cards in places he would find them. All the books told me to do this. I enjoyed it but it seemed like he could have cared less.

Joel had me convinced that everything was my fault and that if I would just get "right" then our marriage would be great... After all, he was the "knight in shining armor!" I just did not **appreciate** all that he was doing for us.

> **JOEL HAD ME CONVINCED THAT EVERYTHING WAS MY FAULT AND THAT IF I WOULD JUST GET "RIGHT" THEN OUR MARRIAGE WOULD BE GREAT.**

Joel would go on an extended fast a couple of times each year. Every time, God would speak to him first **about me!** He would tell Joel that he needed to spend more time with me and be more sensitive. This would only impact Joel for about three days! As soon as I expressed a need for time, affection, attention or a listening ear he would back up. When I would tell him how I felt he would eventually explode and convince me that I was too needy.

Joel and I went together on one of these fasting and prayer getaways to celebrate our anniversary. There was a beautiful castle in Franklin, Pennsylvania that was available for pastors' use. It was supposed to be a time for

Joel and me to enjoy only us: no ministry, no interruptions, and no television. Somehow when we got there, Joel came across a T.V. He convinced me to watch one half-hour comedy. Two days later at the end of our trip all that we could say was that we had watched a lot of television!

This hurt me deeply and we ended up getting in one of those big fights. The Word teaches that when a commitment is broken, a door is opened for the enemy. I informed Joel that because he had broken his commitment to me the enemy had gotten in.

I stood firm and he uncharacteristically accepted responsibility for our blown weekend and the ensuing fight that resulted. God later spoke to Joel during his devotions. He sheepishly shared the verse with me from Proverbs that God used to convict him.

It is a snare for a man to devote something as holy,
and afterward to reconsider his vows.
Proverbs 20:25

Joel had made a promise and broken his word. Every once in a while, at times like this, I would have glimmers of hope for our marriage!

I hated church social events in our first pastorate. We would both work hard to get things ready and be great entertainers but every time Joel would find something to put me down about in front of everyone. It never failed. At some time in that fun event I would get embarrassed or humiliated by a put down.

The four years that immediately followed the adultery were the most difficult years for me. Joel's controlling nature and lack of sensitivity continued to keep our marriage on pins and needles. It was during this time that the grace and peace of God in my life was greatly tested.

Did I ever feel like quitting? You bet! There were many times I thought I was going to **have** to leave concluding, "Enough is enough." But I had the dream, the vision, the prophetic word that **God** had spoken and **I could not let it go. It broke my heart to think that God's dream for us might not come to pass.** If we had been exposed to better information, our bad years could have been shortened. At that point in our history, I only had the "wives should just pray for, submit to and respect their husbands" message. This wrong message (that Joel loved) extended our misery.

I did not ever consider Joel to be physically abusive. The abuse was mental, emotional and spiritual. What is "spiritual abuse?" Spiritual abuse is when a man uses the Word of God to justify mistreatment of his wife. Instead of being gentle and kind toward his wife, he is harsh and condemning. He uses the popular submission scriptures to justify this harsh treatment and keep his wife "under his thumb."

Joel discovered that he could use the Word to justify his inflicting emotional abuse upon and playing mental head games with me. I called Joel my "iron fist." The iron fist would come down anytime I disagreed with him or asked him to treat me with respect.

The solution to spiritual abuse is found in Colossians 3:12-13. "Put on tender mercies, kindness, humility, meekness, longsuffering; bearing with one another and forgiving one another." The solution is simple, yet seemingly an unattainable goal for a spiritually abusive man to implement in his relationship toward his wife.

I lived for years being reminded regularly that the man is the head of the home and that I had to submit to him if I was going to live according to the Word of God. "Anything that he says goes."

> I LIVED FOR YEARS BEING REMINDED REGULARLY THAT THE MAN IS THE HEAD OF THE HOME AND THAT I HAD TO SUBMIT TO HIM.

There was no talk of mutual submission as the Word of God teaches. If I questioned Joel's authority and position as head of our home then I was that **"nagging wife** and **dripping faucet"** that Proverbs **warned** him about!

Abuse can be physical, mental, emotional, sexual or spiritual. You can be controlled in many ways. **We escaped** an abusive marriage. Divorce was not the answer. My "standing" forever like a helpless puppy was not the answer. The life that we **now live** is the answer! The information we share in this book has the ability to lead you out of any abusive tendencies that might be occurring in your marriage.

In those four years following the exposure of the adultery I had to depend on the Holy Spirit more than ever. I was determined that God was going to move on my behalf. Joel **could** find a place of complete repentance from the adultery. God could **use this sin** to **make Joel look at himself** and realize that he had some serious "control freak" character flaws to deal with.

I knew that I had to have a game plan. The Word of God tells us that God's people are destroyed for a lack of knowledge. I decided we were not going to be destroyed. Our family was going to come out on the other side smelling like roses. We were going to make it. We were **not** going to be one of the millions of divorced homes in America.

Recent statistics reveal that divorce in the Christian community is higher than among unbelievers. You don't have to be a part of this statistic. Decide right now that **your family will make it!** Your husband **will be** the man of your dreams and you **will be** the woman of his. Decide to embrace the fact that God is on your side and that He is a friend who sticks closer than a brother.

God is working for your good at this very moment. He has put together a game plan for you. All you have to do is connect up with heaven's thoughts and work the plan.

**If Kathy can do it then so can you!
If Joel became the man of my dreams then your
husband can become the man of yours!**

During those crisis months and years, I lived "in Him" more than ever. Without Christ we would have never recovered. Had we not recovered, we would not have a relationship that God uses to heal other marriages. This is why we are putting our story in written form. What the devil intended for evil God has truly turned around to use for His good.

The devil had his way and now we are making him pay! The deep waters that we have come through equipped us to minister to your marriage. We can help you. The Holy Spirit can take the words that we share and radically revolutionize the life that you share together.

> **THE MORE THAT YOUR HUSBAND LOVES AND VALUES YOU, THE MORE YOU WILL WANT TO DO FOR HIM IN RETURN.**

We teach husbands to love their wives as Christ loves the church and gave his life. For the sake of discussion, I am going to assume that your husband will read this book and "buy into" the ideas we present. If he starts to change before your very eyes, what will you do?

You may have been very hurt and you may not want to trust. You might not believe that the changes your husband is going through are real. This is a normal reaction. It may be a while before you begin to trust again. It took six months before I believed that what I was experiencing was real. While we were in Colorado, God had given me a vision of an apple seed. This represented the great work he had begun in Joel.

Would that seed grow on its own? No! When God says **He** is going to do something, He often means that He will **help you** do it! I had a part to play by responding to the changes that God was working in Joel. As I responded to the changes that were occurring in him, God made additional changes in me.

Christ laid his life down for the church. As we respond by giving our lives to Him He is able to work in us and make us the bride He needs us to be. Marriage works in this same way. As your husband loves you unconditionally, laying his life down for you, it is easy for you to respond positively.

Men are surprised when we tell them that their wives' few issues will go away when they become the husbands that their wives need them to be.

Joel did not like this concept at all. He was convinced that I was at the root of all of our relationship problems.

When Joel bought into this concept and began to change he found out that the concept was true. The issues he previously had with me magically disappeared! All that I did was respond to the changes he was making while not holding a grudge over past injustices.

It is not enough to know that Christ died. We have to embrace what Christ did for us in order for us to benefit. Christ died on the cross to gain the world and by responding to Him we gain an entrance to heaven.

In the same manner I have to find it in my heart to **respond** to my husband. If your husband reads this book and cooperates with the Holy Spirit he will be changing into the **husband** that **you** need him to be. This is the only way he can become the **man** that **God** has called him to be.

How do you respond? One way is to respond by doing the things that please him.

What pleases **your** husband? Does he like it when you make him coffee or cook him breakfast? Maybe he likes it when you give him a back rub or run his bath water. Maybe he would really appreciate it if you cleaned out his car or helped him with some business work.

Doing things that you know please him is a way of responding to the changes God is making in him.

The more that your husband loves and values you, the more you will **want** to do for him in return. You are getting what you want and he is getting what he wants! Now **there** is a formula for a dream marriage!

When we were first married, I really wanted our relationship to be one made in heaven and I tried anything and everything to keep it that way. The *Total Woman* book suggested that I leave sexy notes for my husband. What a brainstorm! I put a note on the outside of our front door waiting to greet Joel when he returned home.

The note read, "Come on in my tall, dark and handsome man." Joel is 5'10", which is not really

54

considered tall, but he does have dark red hair and he is handsome.

While awaiting his return, I fell asleep on the couch. Suddenly I awakened to a knock at the door. There he was! A tall, dark haired, handsome man: the UPS delivery man!

After I signed for the package, he offered that he would have to take me up on my offer next time! Forgetting about the note and confused by his response, I said "Oh, okay!" I went in and lay back down on the couch when suddenly this horrifying thought hit me, "The Note!"

THERE HE WAS! A TALL, DARK HAIRED, HANDSOME MAN: THE UPS DELIVERY MAN!

I ran to the door, just to have it confirmed. There it was in plain sight for the world (and the UPS man) to see! Totally embarrassed, I removed it from the door, went inside and broke up laughing.

It had never crossed my mind that someone else would come to the door! All I wanted to do was add some excitement to Joel's day. The way it turned out was that the excitement intended for Joel was added to the **UPS man's** day! This still gets a great laugh in our home when we recall the incident.

I am quite sure that our house was one that this particular UPS man did not soon forget!

Another way that you can respond to your husband is to get involved in some things that he likes to do. Like most men, Joel enjoys watching football games. Is your husband a football fanatic? Don't be resentful about the football season! Join in! Watch a game or two with him each week! Learn the sport!

I learned the sport and have enjoyed it so much that Monday Night Football has become a much-anticipated private date for us with all of the popcorn, cheese and cracker trimmings! As Hank Williams Jr. sings every Monday night by way of introduction, "Are you ready for some football? A Monday night tradition!"

We **really** enjoy the Super Bowl. We make it into a big church party complete with as many friends and family as possible, along with anyone else we can drag in off the street! We have a great time shouting, cheering, laughing and having an all around great time.

Some things are just not worth fussing over!

GOLDEN KEY

RESPOND WARMLY AND POSITIVELY TO ANY EFFORT YOUR HUSBAND MAKES TOWARD IMPROVING YOUR MARRIAGE.

Dear Joel and Kathy,

Not too long ago I had no hope for our marriage. I can honestly say that Kenneth and I had both come to the point of calling it quits. There were so many times that loneliness seemed to be the only way of life. I felt like everything I said was wrong.

We would argue sometimes for hours. Our fights always ended with bitterness and frustration. I would at times throw things at him in anger. I always felt like the fight was my fault. I could never understand why we just didn't seem to like each other. Many times during our fights I would tell Kenneth that I wanted a divorce. That made things more hopeless.

It was after 12 years of marriage that Kenneth left our three beautiful children and me. I honestly thought that our relationship had ended.

Through a series of events, Kenneth returned home, but our marriage grew even worse. Kenneth threatened to leave again if I did not "straighten up". In the midst of our nightmare, your book landed in Kenneth's hands. I was the first to read it. I was so excited. I knew Kenneth just had to read the book. Knowing his attitude, I told him that the book spoke to women as well as to men. Sure enough, Kenneth read the book in order to find out what I was doing wrong! After Kenneth read the first 100 pages, the change was immediate, lasting and real.

Well I can say that miracles do take place! I never thought this miracle would happen this side of heaven.

I really do not know why it took us so long to finally find our place in this marriage. Instead of having a husband who hates me, I have a husband who is starting to understand me. Instead of having a husband who gets offended at nearly everything I say, I have a husband who actually listens and reassures me when I am upset.

Your book told Kenneth that if he actually listened to me and stopped getting offended, that I would not react the way I have in the past and a lot of my problems would go away. This could not have been a more truthful insight.

It was just today that I was feeling insecure about something. Kenneth came to me and told me that everything was going to be ok and he held me until I felt better. There was a day when he would have told me how wrong I was for feeling that way. Things would have elevated to a fight. Kenneth now understands that it is my heartfelt need to be heard and understood. It is not a need for him to fix me. In the past Kenneth would have felt threatened and taken it personally; now it is not that way.

It is this kind of love coming from him that makes me feel like I can handle life. It is this kind of love that helps me to be the kind of person that my husband needs me to be.

Joel and Kathy, I just want to thank you for what your book has done for our marriage. It is like I have a new husband who really cares for me and says nice things to me. Kenneth has taken his place as the head of our household. He is truly becoming the man of my dreams! Now I have the love that I always needed, to be the women I always knew that I could be... "The Woman of His Dreams!" We're walking in a miracle!

Forever grateful,
Christine Robinson, Tulsa, Oklahoma

Authors' Note
Kenneth and Christine were one of the first couples to receive a copy of the very first manuscript of "The Man of Her Dreams / The Woman of His!" Their copy was an e-mail attachment which required downloading, saving and printing from their computer. They read the book in September of 2004. They continue to live a miracle marriage in 2008.

Chapter Five

What Would Her Answer Be?

By Joel

"Does your husband love you?"
What would your wife's answer be?

What would your wife's answer be if her best girlfriend asked this question of her in strict confidence? I am **not asking** you what her answer would be if she were fielding this question from **you** or your **pastor** or one of your **mutual** close friends. What would her answer be if her best friend asked her this when they were out shopping and she felt truly safe that you would never hear her answer?

Does that make you nervous?

Would her answer be "Oh yes, he loves me so much and he shows it to me every day! He is so wonderful! You would just not believe how attentive he is to my needs and how he is always complimenting me. I am always his first priority and he loves to be with me."

"I can talk to him about anything; when he treats me poorly I simply have to mention it. He immediately apologizes and tries to avoid repeating it. We always give each other love touches. We really enjoy making love as often as possible and it is enjoyable for both of us. It is as good or better now than when we were first married!"

Or would her answer be something along these lines, "Well, yes, my husband loves me in his own way. He may not show it much but you just have to understand my husband! You see he works really hard. He is a steady, dependable husband. We don't do too much fun stuff. Of course we argue regularly like every couple does. We don't make love very often but as 'everyone knows,' sex is not that important after 20 years."

> **IMAGINE WHAT YOUR WIFE'S FANTASIES WERE WHEN SHE WAS A LITTLE GIRL DREAMING ABOUT HER FUTURE HUSBAND. HOW DO YOU THINK HER DREAM MAN BEHAVED?**

"We have worked out a comfortable living arrangement. I am content in that."

If your wife would answer along the lines of the latter options then we have some work to do!

Many men do not have a clue about what it takes to be a husband who makes loving their wife their first priority. A good mental exercise would be for you to imagine what your wife's fantasies were when she was a little girl dreaming about her future husband. How do you think her dream man behaved?

I don't think that her dream husband yelled to get his point across, ignored her feelings, told her she was

60

stupid and/or did not help out around the house. I am pretty sure that her dream husband was loving, caring, attentive, and helpful.

You could imagine that her dream man was a good provider and when money was low he would work hard to find money. Her dream husband listened to her when she shared her thoughts and found her every opinion extremely valuable. She no doubt fantasized about romantic nights, evenings under star-filled skies, walks on the beach and meaningful heart-to-heart communication.

You can fulfill your wife's fantasies. You **can** fulfill her dreams. The best part is that as you are becoming the husband that your wife dreamed about you will notice that she is becoming the wife who you dreamed about! You will find that your wife progressively becomes easier to get along with, fun to be around, helps you accomplish your mutual goals and genuinely enjoys having fun in bed as often as possible!

When I was in elementary school I would notice the attractive, fun loving and care free ladies on the cover of my mother's "Good Housekeeping" magazines and imagined my wife being just like those ladies at 40 years of age. I have that dream wife today and she just turned 44! We have been married 24 years; our marriage keeps improving while Kathy continues to get more beautiful every year! She looks better this year than she has ever looked! Wow!

Over 25 years ago Charlie Shedd taught me in his famous book, *Letters to Phillip*, that if I would treat my wife right she would get better looking every year! Kudos to Charlie Shedd! It works! I treat Kathy wonderfully and in response Kathy has discovered a passion for studying clothes, hair and make-up, which results in her looking and dressing absolutely fabulous! Woo hoo!

We have had some terribly bad times in these 24 years, nine bad years to be exact according to Kathy. These last few years though have been quite spectacular as the principles that we learned at Life Skills in Colorado have taken root and grown into the fabulous life-giving tree that is our marriage.

We want you to eat the fruit from our marriage tree. We want you to taste and see that marriage can be truly exciting and absolutely wonderful. You can still be madly in love with the wife of your youth after 20 or 30 years together. You can recover from adultery, abuse, neglect and abandonment. Everything can be forgiven and you can learn how to be the man that God has called you to be by becoming the husband your wife needs you to be.

Anthony told me that his marriage was miserable. He and Samantha owned two restaurants and they really had no relationship at all. He ran one restaurant while Samantha tended to the second. According to Anthony, divorce seemed to be their only option.

I mentioned to Anthony that Kathy and I did marriage counseling and that I could help him if he would like. He consented to listen so I gave him a 15-minute crash course in marriage. I told him that the reason he had a bad marriage was most likely because he was not listening to his wife and that he probably had quit meeting her needs years ago.

He nodded his head so I continued, "The facts are, Anthony, that men do not have a clue how to meet their sweetheart's needs. Your wife probably gets on your case all the time about things that she thinks you are doing wrong in your relationship doesn't she?" Anthony smiled a bit again, agreeing with my statement.

> I EXPLAINED TO ANTHONY THAT THE WAY FOR A MAN TO QUIT FEELING HEN-PECKED IS TO SIMPLY DO WHAT HIS WIFE ASKS HIM TO DO THE FIRST TIME THAT SHE ASKS.

I then offered this gem. "I bet that you feel hen-pecked, don't you?" This revolutionary insight also received a positive reaction. I explained to Anthony that the way for a man to quit feeling hen-pecked is to simply **do what his wife asks him to do the first time that she asks.**

Most men let their pride get in the way and they resist everything that their wife asks them to do. I told him that his wife desperately wanted a good relationship with him and if he would simply do the things that she has been asking him to do and take time to listen to her heart she would open up to him and their marriage would drastically improve.

Anthony questioned this tactic saying that it sounded like he would be letting his wife be in control of him. I assured him that the opposite would happen. When Anthony met Samantha's needs she would relax and he would not feel at all like she was trying to control him.

I shared with him for a moment how I formerly would resist Kathy's stated needs telling her that they were too deep for me to meet. This tactic would then cause us to get into huge arguments. When I later decided to drop my pride and listen to her heart Kathy miraculously turned into a fabulous wife! I promised him that if he would do as I did he would enjoy the same results in having a happy wife and a more fulfilling marriage.

I did not see Anthony again for six months. I knew he would either be enjoying an improved marriage or that he would be divorced. To my inquiry as to "How's the love life?" Anthony happily reported that he did what I suggested and that he and his wife were getting along really well. I have been in touch with Anthony twice a year and he continues to tell me that they are doing well. Fifteen minutes changed his life.

A year later I stopped at their restaurant and Samantha was acting as hostess. She had a peaceful and relaxed look about her even in the midst of people waiting in line to get a table and a lot of general confusion on the busy night. Knowing that men always think that their marriages are more successful than they really are, I asked Samantha how things were going with Anthony and she also reported that things were going well.

Anthony and Samantha did not read this book. Anthony and Samantha have not been to our marriage seminar nor have they attended our church. Fifteen minutes of **truth** and a **committed response** was the key to saving their marriage and giving them a happy relationship.

A second illustration of how simple this whole thing can be is the conversation that I had recently with a young man after a special church service we had both attended. Ron was neatly dressed and excited about Jesus. He was exuberant over the blessing that he had received from the meeting and was looking to set the world on fire for Jesus. I asked Ron if he was married and he replied that he was divorced.

> **RON WAS "ON FIRE FOR JESUS" AND COMMITTED TO FULFILLING HIS MINISTRY CALL, SO IT WAS PLAIN TO SEE THAT HIS WIFE WAS IN REBELLION.**

With a "sad puppy dog" look he told me that they had been a Christian couple but that his wife left him taking the children with her. At this point his wife and children were in another state some ten hours away! Ron had just spoken with her that day in an effort to get her to be reunited but she refused, telling him that he just needed to get on with his life.

The traditional "Christian" response to this would have been to tell him that I could sympathize with his plight. Seeing how **Ron** was **"on fire for Jesus"** and committed to **"fulfilling his ministry call"** it **was plain to see** that his **wife** was **"in rebellion"** and she was choosing to live in **disobedience to God** by rejecting his request to be reunited.

The "counselor" might have offered a prayer that her heart would be convicted and if she refused the "wooing of the Holy Spirit" that God would bring a **"truly Godly woman"** into Ronald's life who would be a helpmeet to him in **fulfilling his ministry calling.** As an **afterthought** the counselor might add "and show Ron any area that he might need to change in order to be a better husband whether in a reunited marriage or with the next wife that God would bring."

Instead of this, Ron received the sixty-second "Davisson Bomb." Without taking a breath in between sentences I said, "Well, I bet the reason that she left you is that you did not have a clue about how to be a husband. You probably refused to meet her needs, told her to quit harassing you when she simply wanted to share her heart and you probably tried to make her feel like an idiot most of the time. If the truth were to be told it would be that you were the bottom line cause of most of your marriage problems. My guess is that you acted like a child at about the emotional age of five! If you had listened to her heart and met her needs she never would have left you and you would be with your family tonight. Isn't that right?"

As I said this, Ron's eyes grew larger and larger. When I ended he said, "You are right! How did you know all of that? Man, I was like the Tasmanian Devil! I was always screaming and ranting and raving. Anytime she asked anything of me it was like all hell broke loose." I told Ron that he needed to call and "fess up" to his wife.

The only chance Ron has of getting her back would be to convince her that **he truly believes** what she **already knew**. His pride and insecurities were at the root of **all** of their marriage problems. He will have to present to her that he is determined to grow up emotionally and that he would be willing to meet her needs even if he did not understand them.

This was all exchanged in a five-minute meeting in a hotel elevator and lobby with a person that I have never seen again. I don't know the end of the story but if Ron did what I suggested it would not surprise me to discover that he eventually reunited with his family.

Make sure that your wife **knows** that you love her by **listening to her heart** and **meeting her needs**. This way she can give a glowing report when she is asked that soul-searching question,

"Does your husband love you?"

GOLDEN KEY

BEGIN TODAY TO SHOW LOVE IN WAYS THAT ARE UNMISTAKABLE AND UNDENIABLE

THE DEFINITION OF INSANITY
(Applied to Daily Life)

It has been said that the definition of insanity is, "Doing the same thing repeatedly and expecting different results, *this* time."

The Body of Christ has been relying on the same basic principles for marriage success since 1960. Some say that it has been even longer than this. Today, the church is reaping the inevitable results of these marriage teachings: The divorce rate is reported to be over 50%, exceeding the divorce rate found even among non-Christians.

If you continue to follow these traditional marriage teachings that have been popular in the Body of Christ, you have a 50/50 chance (or less) of surviving "until death do us part". Imagine for a moment all of the Christian couples that you know today that appear to be happily married.

Do you see them in your mind's eye? They appear happy, don't they? Divorce does not seem inevitable. If they were to divorce, you would be shocked, remarking, "I didn't even know that they were having problems." Now, stop and realize that, according to statistics, half of these marriages will end in divorce. The hopes and dreams of their wedding day will end in ashes if something drastic does not occur to change this destiny.

The Body of Christ appears to be the embodiment of this definition of insanity when it comes to marriage teaching. The church clings tenaciously to the same traditional marriage teachings that have failed repeatedly, in the hopes that, though they have failed miserably to create happy marriages for over 45 years, perhaps *this time* they will succeed.

If you look carefully into the Christian marriages that **have** lasted forty, fifty or sixty years, you will discover that in many of these "successful" marriages, one or both partners are not really very happy. Many have stayed in these unhappy, unfulfilled relationships simply because they know that God hates divorce. Yes, they have survived… but that is a long way from being outrageously happy. They are not experiencing the glory of God in their marriage. Their relationship is not a taste of "heaven on earth". They have simply surrendered to the doldrums of an unfulfilled life, resigned to a marriage that never met their joyous expectations. Their dreams have given way to quiet sadness.

Oftentimes, when longtime married couples are asked about the state of their marital happiness, the husband will offer simply that, "Well, we have been married for 45 years… we must be doing something right." The non-response of the wife, combined with her somewhat stressed countenance communicates the real answer.

Thank God for the few couples who represent the small percentage of marriages that have succeeded in living truly happy and successful marriages. These are the exception. We believe that these special couples have happy marriages not *because* of traditional marriage teachings but *in spite* of them. A happy marriage was easy for them. It just came natural. These special couples would have had a happy marriage without ever reading one marriage book or attending one marriage seminar.

These long-term, successful and truly happy marriages represent about 10% of all Christian couples. The other 90% of us either were or are currently **victims** of the flawed marriage emphases we were offered when we went searching for answers.

We have good news for you. We have found the answer for this struggling 90%. The answer is not more of the same re-packaged teachings that have been popular for these many years. The answer is a totally new paradigm. Why can we say this? We can say this because we learned the hard way. We tried the traditional approach for the first ten years of our marriage. And we experienced frustrations, disappointment and miseries that may have resembled those you have experienced. Yes, like you, we had some happy times. Yes, we also had some seasons where we got along well. But our happy times were not long lasting and we had to work really hard to attain those short-lived joyful "seasons" in our marriage.

On the other hand, for the last 14 years of our 24-year marriage, we have been living this same new paradigm that we are encouraging you to embrace. Thanks to it, we have been experiencing an outrageously happy "season" of happiness for over a decade now... And it is easy once the new paradigm is embraced.

If you are single today or you are newlywed, you have choices. You can build your future on the same traditions that have felled so many before you, you can just let the chips fall where they may, or you can build your future on the basis of a paradigm that works.

Hear us loud and clear: A happy marriage is so very, very, very easy... by adopting the new and fresh paradigm that God taught us.

A happy marriage is hard, and a happy marriage is easy. It is a paradox. Embracing this new paradigm takes dying to self for a husband. It demands that he become a servant. This is excruciatingly hard for a short time, as the flesh never enjoys the dying process. Dying to self is hard, but after you die, living is easy. *After* the seed has fallen into the ground and died, it brings forth much fruit. The new life that results from death to self, pride and ego brings forth a wonderfully harmonious and happy marriage relationship.

This fresh paradigm has been available all along, contained in the pages of the New Testament, waiting to be discovered by a church that would finally become desperate enough to cry out for answers and be willing to give God's way a chance when it is discovered.

Some husbands will receive this new paradigm with joy. To these men, discovering the keys to a happy marriage is more important than protecting their insecurities, inferiority and pride. If you are married to one of these men, you are fortunate indeed. On the other hand, a small percentage of men will react harshly against it and stubbornly cling to tradition. If this is you, we offer our compassion. You have only a 50/50 chance of making it... and if you make it, you have about a 10% chance of ever having an outrageously happy marriage. Those are not good odds, but if you choose to take that gamble, we send our prayers and hopes that you will be one of those few who miraculously "stumble upon" a happy marriage.

On the other hand, we are presenting you with a fresh opportunity to discover and enjoy that elusive, happy marriage. If you, as a couple, will "buy into" this new marriage paradigm, our promise to you is that your chance of success and happiness as a couple will be almost 100%. The testimonies found in the pages of this book from other couples (just like you) whose marriages have been dramatically changed for the better are proof that if a husband and wife will embrace what God has taught us, they will experience the same happy results in their marriage as God has given to us.

Dear Joel and Kathy,

My mother has just left my father after 45 years of marriage! She said that after reading your book a couple of times she realized she was not to blame for the problems in the marriage. She really grasped every word that was written.

It helped her toughen up and take a stand against the emotional and spiritual abuse of my father. (He is an assistant pastor of a non-denominational church.) He says one thing in the pulpit and another thing at home. I am so proud of my mother for taking a stand. Right now she is staying in a motel, and she and my father are talking things through.

This is all good! Praise God for your story.

TEN DAYS LATER...

You are not going to believe this! My mom stayed in the motel for one week. Dad read the book during that week and God took the scales off his eyes. He is a changed man and is willing to testify to this fact in front of the whole church and also his children. They are going to renew their vows February 13, reception and all. Dad went out and bought mom a whole set of rings and a wedding dress! This is too awesome!

What an awesome God we serve!

ONE MONTH LATER...

My folks are doing great! Mom said dad is like a little kid in a candy store...

God Bless,
Allyssa Monroe, Alabama

ONE WEEK AFTER THE CEREMONY...

Dear Joel and Kathy,

Mom and dad had a beautiful ceremony, Unity candle and all. They also took communion, just the two of them! All five of us children were in it, too; we lit our candles to represent our birth order, and our family unit. There were a couple of songs sung, and then the pastor told the congregation that in all 30 years of preaching, he had never seen a transformation like my father has made!

Dad told the congregation that he will never raise his voice in anger to mom ever again. He said he had the knowledge of the Bride of Christ in his head all these years but didn't have it in his heart. Once it made it to his heart, he understood how he was supposed to treat my mom. There were two wedding cakes, bride and groom's cake, gifts and a honeymoon, too. Because my husband works at a resort, we were able to get them a two-bedroom condo for one night (with a fireplace). All of us kids pitched in and gave them money to pay for their room and going out to eat.

After they had checked into their room and went out to eat, my husband and I drove to the resort and had the front desk take to their room a food basket with all kinds of goodies that I had put together: chocolates, cheese, grapes, sausages, and a candle.

They are on cloud nine! Praise God! I went ahead and gave my other two brothers each a book for Valentine's Day. Now my sister and all my brothers have your book. I can't keep them! My mom cleans my house and was here yesterday and took two, one to give to a woman at her church and one to give to her biological sister. They are going like hotcakes around here! I'll be ordering more when their testimony is in your next edition. You guys have no idea how many lives you have touched.

God Bless,
Allyssa Monroe

Chapter Six

Rate Your Marriage
On A Scale of 1–10

By Joel

How do you rate your marriage on a scale of 1–10? How would your wife rate your marriage? This is your starting point. The only way to measure the current state of your marriage is to honestly evaluate it.

More than likely, your wife will be wary of this exercise. Chances are that when talking about your relationship she has been met with a deaf ear, ridicule, arguments or justifications.

In order to get an **honest** evaluation from your wife you must guarantee her a "safe place". There are three places that must be safe in life: family, church and friendships. In most homes it is not safe for the wife to tell her husband that she is unhappy in their relationship. Begin by assuring her that you would like an honest estimation of your marriage in order to work on **your** issues that might be contributing to any discord in your relationship.

Most men will rate their marriages about a 7-9 on a scale of 1-10. Their wives will normally rate **the same marriage** a 5-7! This is completely normal. Women spend a lot more time "feeling" about their marriage relationship than men do.

The husband/associate pastor in the testimony that you just read had no idea how unhappy his wife had been for 45 years. Men often compartmentalize their lives. A man can section off any problems in his marriage relationship and focus on other things he wants to conquer such as his job or a hobby. He might realize that there are unsolved issues but he can get a self-image boost from his other activities.

The wife on the other hand does not section these things off as well. If there are issues that have not been brought to closure they stay with her. In her mind the whole marriage is difficult because of the unsolved issue. She is incredulous that hubby can just go on to other interests in life while she is left frustrated.

> SHE IS INCREDULOUS THAT HUBBY CAN JUST GO ON TO OTHER INTERESTS IN LIFE WHILE SHE IS LEFT FRUSTRATED.

When our family was on the road full time for the purpose of recovery after the adultery we had opportunity to eat out often and enjoy family activities. I was in sales work at the time.

I could not understand why Kathy was not being lighthearted, carefree and happy. This was very frustrating to me and caused many arguments.

We both remember the day at Sea World when I looked at Kathy and said, "What is wrong with you?

These should be the happiest days of our lives. We are on the road as a family full time, living in hotels, eating in restaurants and today we are at Sea World. Why do you have 'that look?'" (All men know what "that look" is. It is the look that is announcing that our sweetheart is not very happy right now.)

The bottom line was that I was unwilling to give Kathy closure on some issues and I would not allow her to bring the subjects up without it turning into a big blowout. She was carrying these things in her heart. It was easy for me to forbid her to bring touchy subjects up, close my heart and be as happy as a bluebird on a summer day!

For at least a full year after the adultery my heart was still affected by the soul tie. The other woman was still in my heart and Kathy knew it. I insisted on periodic get-togethers with the other couple. This would prove that all that happened was forgiven. We could still be best friends. (Immaturity never wants to feel the consequences for sin. This is also why I initially wanted to stay in the pulpit.)

Women are sensitive by nature. Kathy knew that my heart was divided and this affected her in the depths of her heart. Kathy would express her need for closure asking me to quit insisting that we all get together occasionally. I could not simply say to her, "I understand. I hurt you deeply in the worst possible way. As far as husbands go, I am the worst of the low. I promise you a safe place. We will never get together with the other couple unless you want us to, because you know that the soul tie in me is not broken."

I could not do this simple thing. I had to be in control. I had to keep Kathy off balance. I would tell her that she was ridiculous and wrong to "hold onto her pain." I forbade her to bring the subject up. It was classic control and manipulation emanating from unwillingness on my part to embrace her pain.

I refused to give Kathy a safe place to share her heart, her hurts and especially her deeply felt feelings. It was easier to just tell her that everything she said and felt was wrong.

If **you** also have a history of telling **your wife** why she is wrong when she tries to talk to you, she may not be forthcoming. If you have a chip on your shoulder and she thinks from past experiences that you might scream at her for giving the marriage a "2", you probably won't hear the truth. If previously you have argued with her and tried to convince her that she did not perceive things correctly then you are probably going to have a difficult time getting a straight answer.

Why would she want to get into yet **another** argument over your relationship? Amy simply gave up. Every time that Don and Amy went to marriage counseling they ended up in an argument. Even the counselor suggested that she not try to talk to Don. Don had done a fabulous job convincing the counselor that Amy was wrong about everything, so she was told to "just not say anything and ask God to speak to him."

Do whatever you have to do in order to convince your wife that it is safe to be honest with you and then keep your word. Don't argue. Don't demand to know why she is grading it a "2". Just accept her answer and continue reading, knowing that you have a lot to work on! If your wife tells you that your grade is a "9", let me suggest that she might be afraid to be honest with you.

Tom, a young minister in Ohio asked Becky this question. He related the outcome to me: "My wife and I were lying on the couch cuddling and I asked her how she would rate our marriage on a scale of 1-10. She told me that she rates it a 9."

At the time, Tom was unemployed. Though he has a call on his life, there had been no progress in his ministry. His days and nights were spent at home except for the times that he did street ministry. His family had never been able to stay in a church because he would not commit to a local church and a pastor. His wife and children had been the ones who had suffered.

Since Tom did not work and did not believe in tithing even if he were committed to a local church, financial pressures were huge. At times Becky had not even been able to afford gas to get their son to his regularly scheduled medical appointments. Becky had confided in close friends that Tom just wanted too much attention. The children needed her and Tom needed her. Becky spent her days with all of the demands of their three children and when she was emotionally spent Tom wanted her to fill his very deep emotional cup.

My exposure to their relationship had been limited but on one occasion I saw them disagree. Tom blew up, verbally berated Becky and told her that she needed to "get back in the house." It was very humiliating for me to even watch. It was obvious that when there was a disagreement the iron fist would come out and Becky was "put into her place."

With this backdrop, Tom chose a moment when they were cuddling to ask the question; a time that he knew she **could only** answer one way safely. Sure enough, Becky told Tom that she would rate their marriage a "9". I don't think so. Becky, like many women, could not answer this question honestly. A wife knows when her man is so insecure that if she does not "butter his bread" he will explode in a display of hurt, anger, demands or justifications.

> **IT WAS OBVIOUS THAT WHEN THERE IS A DISAGREEMENT THE IRON FIST COMES OUT AND BECKY IS "PUT INTO HER PLACE."**

This is the first step in finding God's answer to that all-important question: "How do I become the man that God has called me to be?" Your goal is to have a wife that is so happy that she will **honestly** rate your marriage a 9 or 10. There is a happy ending to Becky and Tom's story. A series of events coincided to bring change. Becky kicked Tom out. Tom read this book. At some point, Tom came to a place of change. Today, they have a happy marriage, Tom works hard and he has matured greatly.

Joe really did not think that he had any areas that he needed to change in. As a member of our church he reported weekly to us on all of the problems that his wife was causing. Finally we met with Liz. We made a list of some of the things that Joe had wanted her to do. Liz was agreeable to this. We then asked her to list 10 things that she had been asking Joe to do differently in their marriage. These things had been ignored.

When we presented her requests to Joe, his face went ashen. "Joe, has Liz presented these requests to you before?" "Yes." "Have you been doing them?" "No." "Are you the same Mr. Perfect who has been telling us that you are doing everything while your wife is at fault for everything?" "Well, I uh, uh…"

If you can't see that you are at fault, ask a trusted couple to sit down with your wife and pick her brain for you! Let them request from your wife a list of ten things that you can do to improve your marriage. The chances are that you will recognize all ten requests from previous conversations and arguments!

This is not a one or two-week "fixer-upper" process. This will take time. You might see some immediate progress depending on the current state of your relationship.

Your genuine care and effort at improving your marriage will lift your wife's emotional load. If you do not see immediate improvement then that may be a signal that your wife does not yet trust your good intentions. Be patient.

There are some things that you can do that are very easy to help the process. Shining your crown is a good place to start. Compliment your wife, build her up, praise her and be sure that she realizes that you value her over friends, hobbies, work or ministry. Her value cannot consist of, "After Bible study, after prayer, after work, after church; if there is any time left we will spend that together."

> **COMPLIMENT YOUR WIFE, BUILD HER UP, PRAISE HER AND BE SURE THAT SHE REALIZES THAT YOU VALUE HER OVER FRIENDS, HOBBIES, WORK OR MINISTRY.**

Embrace the Word that God spoke to me nine years ago. "When you spend time with your wife and children you are spending time with Me. How can you say that you love Me whom you cannot see if you cannot love your wife and children whom you can see?" (Chapter 13 is entitled "Shining Your Crown")

Do your really want a marriage that is outrageously happy? Do you really want a marriage that is like heaven on earth? If you really want this, if you are really committed, you are taking the first steps. You are communicating. You are listening. You are changing. You are changing in your actions and you are changing in your attitudes. Your inner man is being challenged to grow.

The hard changes are these inner changes affecting your core being. They are actually changing who you are as a person. These changes are touching those places inside that are insecure, protected by a wall of pride and ego. The rubber will meet the road when you realize that there are things that your wife has been telling you for years that were met with a deaf ear. This can be humiliating. How about giving in on an argument even if you think that you are right? These are the difficult places.

If you truly want to take the first step in marriage improvement and/or restoration you will have to somehow convince your wife that her honest rating of your marriage will not incite a riot or a cold war in your household! Let her know that you really **want** to begin working on improving your weak areas. Assure her that you can only do this is if she is totally, perhaps even brutally honest.

Tell her you are going to be a big boy and take your medicine without arguing, justifying, berating or accusing! If you can get your wife to open up then you will have successfully completed step one on this road to marital bliss!

GOLDEN KEY

RATE YOUR MARRIAGE
ON A SCALE OF 1-10.
ASK YOUR WIFE TO DO THE SAME.
COMPARE SCORES.

PERSONALITY-SPECIFIC?

Your personalities are unique. It **does not matter** what personalities you and your spouse have. The principles found in *The Man of Her Dreams/The Woman of His!* automatically customize themselves to your individual marriage and unique personalities. Let's explore how.

From Joel to the men: Your wife might have a completely different personality than that of Kathy. You might have a totally different personality than mine. However, regardless of your personality or that of your wife, I can assure you that your wife has needs that God is calling upon you to discover, appreciate and fulfill. In the bad days, I did not want to meet Kathy's needs. To meet her needs, I would have to die to my ego and pride and grow and mature as a man. The old nature in man has an in-bred aversion to fulfilling his wife's needs. The way that you grow into the new man that God has called you to be is to become the husband that YOUR wife needs YOU to be. You must meet YOUR wife's specific, heartfelt needs. Personality has nothing to do with it.

Perhaps *your* wife wants you to be more of a leader. Perhaps she says to you that she would like for you to take the lead on Sunday mornings and take the *entire family* to church, *every* week. Instead, you *sleep in on Sundays* like a bump on a log. This is *your wife's* personal need that you have to fulfill in order to grow into the man that God has called *you* to become. Kathy and I never had this problem. Our problem was that I was *too much* the leader. (Correction: Control-Freak.) I was a *control-freak* because I was acting like an eight-year-old. *You* lay in bed on Sunday mornings, *refusing* to take the family to church because *you* are acting like an eight-year-old! Grow up!

Maybe your wife asks you to have a time each day where *you* lead the family in prayer and share in a family Bible reading time. Instead, you engage the remote control. (This would be acting at what emotional age? Hmm. Perhaps *five* years old?)

From Kathy to the ladies: If you ask your husband to lead a prayer and Bible reading time and he agrees to do so, every night at 7 pm, then here is your challenge. At 7 pm tomorrow night, your husband's flesh might be getting the victory. You look into the living room and he is comfortably situated for what appears to be a long night of TV watching! It is apparent that he has completely forgotten about this new commitment, or he might be feeling lazy and is hoping that you have forgotten all about it. But, he read this book, and he *did* agree to lead the family altar hour. So, now, what do you do? Are you ready for this? You *help him* keep his promise! How? Hand him a Bible and gently remind him, with a cup of tea and a kiss, that it is time for the family prayer and Bible reading time. Turn the TV off and call the kids in. Sit next to him and joyfully say, "Okay, man of God! Lead the way! Start the praying!" Please, ladies, *do not* just be disappointed that your husband is being defeated by his flesh and *silently stew* while the evening passes without his leading a family worship time. If you do, you will *probably* have a blowout after a few days. This would not be healthy. Your husband will get strong in time. For now he is weak. This is all new. Prime the pump! Help him! *Nicely, please.* What are you after? You are after a positive result. Gently reminding your husband and *leading him into* being a leader, if necessary, is not wrong. If hubby gets mad at you for reminding and gently pushing him, he is acting like a child and needs to read this book... again!

From Joel to the men: Kathy and I are both very vocal. When Kathy would present her needs to me in "the bad days," I would resist her verbal "presentation." The results were aggressive, unpleasant and sometimes very loud. You, on the other hand, might be the "strong, silent type" (or just the silent type). When *your* wife presents *her* needs to you, *you* might respond by *withdrawing* and *ignoring* her. Your wife could get loud, animated, come unglued, and what do *you* do? Why, you just *sit there, staring straight ahead,* looking like Mr. Perfect! Perhaps you keep your eyes closed or hide behind a newspaper. But inside you are steaming. "Look at my wife. She is flipping out. Why doesn't she just *leave me alone*? If she *thinks* that *I* am going to be 'sensitive to her feelings' when *she* is acting like *this*, she is *sadly mistaken*. I am just going to sit here and do *nothing*. She will not move *me*!" You might hum, "I shall, I shall, *I shall not* be moved!"

As your wife is bouncing off the walls, so to speak, and finally leaves the room, slamming the door behind her, you settle more firmly into your seat or couch and reach for the remote. You are convinced that she is the entire problem in your marriage. You have *no intention* of listening to her heart, appreciating and validating her feelings or meeting her stated needs. To make matters worse, you REALLY BELIEVE that she is the problem, when you yourself are actually the culprit. The problem with denial is that when you are in it, you do not know it! If you did, you would not be in denial. You **really believe** that your wife is the root of your problems. If she would just get a grip and leave you alone, you would not be having these "scenes". You are firmly entrenched in denial, you believe the story, and you are sticking to it!

What is really going on? Your wife is making a request of you, and your insecurities and pride and immaturity emotionally repel you away from meeting her need. You refuse to do anything that she asks of you. Like an eight-year-old in an adult body, you have put your foot down. "I don't care what she says. I will not do what she asks." You are reacting out of the same old nature that I reacted from when I refused to meet Kathy's needs and proceeded to demand loudly that she leave me alone. The only difference is that your weapon is your silence. Your personality is different. The sin nature, though, is the same. Every man struggles with the same "old man."

Your perfectly executed delay produces **exactly** what you want: Your wife flips out and you are again successful in avoiding any responsibility in helping her. You are very proficient at this. You know exactly how to use your silence to send your wife into hysteria whenever you choose. No one can see the complete and utter defiance that is boiling inside of you toward your wife. All they see is that your wife sometimes appears to be unstable and very unsubmissive. Your wife's yelling is really a form of rebellion to "God's authority." (Those who teach this doctrine of authority are in *grave* error and are sending men into unrestrained power trips.) Suzie has been successfully and expertly manipulated by your silence. This is not mentally healthy for any woman. Suzie takes one step closer to becoming certifiably unstable.

How *should* this have played out? Suzie notices that her new man is lying down, watching TV. She also notes that you have vacuumed the floors. "Thanks for vacuuming the house. That is so sweet. Will you help me bring the groceries in and run a load of dishes while I cook?" Your reply? "It would be *my pleasure*. I *love* you and will do *anything* to *be a blessing* to you" as you give her a kiss and a hug. Suzie beams with pride over how wonderful you are. After you help with the groceries, Suzie says, "You know what? Never mind. You are *so sweet*. Why don't you go and lie back down on the couch and relax. I will cook dinner, and load the dishes myself. You can help unload them after we eat." See how easy this is? No yelling! No counseling sessions! But you have to grow up. You have to be dead to self. Your pride has to be gone. Dying is hard and then it is very easy. Being a servant is hard, and then it is very, very easy. Meeting your wife's needs is hard, and then it is very, very easy. This is why having a happy marriage is hard and yet very, very easy. This is the paradox.

Chapter Seven

Your Personal Marriage Manual

Likewise, ye husbands, **dwell with them according to knowledge, giving honor unto the wife** *as unto the weaker vessel and as being heirs together of the grace of life* **that your prayers** *be not hindered.*

I Peter 3:7

By Joel

Live with your wife according to knowledge,
so that **your prayers** *will not be hindered.*

God has equipped every woman with a marriage manual in her heart, which is custom designed to instruct her husband in how to meet her individual and unique needs. A man who can learn how to tap into this marriage manual and heed its instructions will have all of the information needed on how to have heaven on earth in his marriage.

God did not give this marriage manual to men. A man is basically born without a clue as to how to meet his wife's needs. You are reading this book, which probably means you have a desire to experience a good marriage. The goal of this book is really to help you to turn your heart toward your wife and be willing to become the husband she needs you to be by listening to her heart.

Many wives are quite vocal. For the first few years of marriage they will attempt to communicate to their husbands what it is that they need from them in order to feel loved. The problem many times is that the husband thinks that he knows what is best for the marriage! Perhaps he **has** read some books on marriage. Perhaps he understands some **general** principles of marriage that have helped **other couples.** Thinking he knows how to meet his wife's needs, he begins to feel like his wife is attempting to manipulate him when she shares her heart with him. After years of trying to communicate her desires a wife will finally give up.

> **GOD HAS EQUIPPED EVERY WOMAN WITH A MARRIAGE MANUAL IN HER HEART, DESIGNED TO INSTRUCT HER HUSBAND IN HOW TO MEET HER UNIQUE NEEDS.**

Each wife is unique and she has the manual for her **own** marriage. I was very proud of all of the marriage books I read before marrying Kathy. She was thrilled to marry a guy who seemed interested in having a great relationship. The problem came after we were married and Kathy began to express what she needed from me individually.

If it were not my idea, I would resist! If she wanted to talk, I would buy her flowers. If she wanted to get some flowers, I would take her out to dinner. I was insistent that Kathy be grateful and thankful for the expressions of love that I wanted to show to her instead of listening and responding to her heart.

Controlling husbands can often be considered "great guys" to onlookers and even to their wives. They can be charming, romantic, good providers, they can go out of their way to do nice things and at times they can be extremely attentive. I was all of these, when **I** wanted to be.

Kathy and I had many good times. We would go on dates, play cards and visit family and friends together. We also did a variety of team ministries. I would put sincere effort into making Kathy happy. Flowers, gifts, compliments… all on my schedule and on my terms. I was committed to meeting Kathy's needs as long as I was the one who decided exactly what her needs were. I wanted to be the hero. After all, in my mind I had "rescued" Kathy from a life of mediocrity and I was determined to give her a life of greatness!

I had studied marriage books and envisioned myself as the ultimate, perfect, heroic, rescuing husband. No ten-year-old little boy envisions himself growing up into a control freak husband! We all think that we will be great husbands. With this attitude I had set out to create a great marriage based on what I believed our marriage needed. I was going to be the hero! What I could not do was to simply listen to Kathy's heart and meet the real, heartfelt needs that she expressed. I figured that all of my contributions made up for the needs I did not meet and that Kathy should be grateful.

It's not that Kathy would have wanted me to quit doing all of the surface things that I did to add to our marriage. Every woman enjoys cards, gifts and dinner out.

It is just that every woman needs her man to meet the real needs that she expresses and then she can enjoy all of the extras. I am reminded of Jesus, explaining to the seven churches in Revelation, "You are doing well, but this one thing I have against you." It is not that Jesus was hard to please. He simply knew that they were overlooking the things that were most important. The things that are most important to your wife are the things that make her heart uneasy about how you are treating her. It is the little foxes that spoil the vine.

One time I bought Kathy a new van with this comment, "There, now you know that I love you." In this I demonstrated that sometimes I simply did not have a clue!

My attitude at that time concerning being the rescuing "hero" is not uncommon. Controlling men **often** marry someone who they feel they are "rescuing". They go into marriage with a "hero mentality". They do not consider themselves manipulative or controlling in the least. On the contrary, they consider themselves "protectors". Their abusive nature surfaces later and sometimes surprises even themselves! In the worst cases abuse starts immediately. Other times it takes a year or two to begin manifesting.

Nancy told us that it took three years for her charming, considerate and handsome husband to become physically abusive. The severe abuse started suddenly. It took her by surprise. Nancy had seen the "good" side of her husband and stayed with him much too long in futile hope. Finally, in fear for her life, Nancy packed up her children and whatever belongings she could stuff into her little car and drove off in search of a new life.

Today Nancy is a happily married Christian businesswoman living in the paradise that is called Hilton Head Island. Like all women, all that Nancy ever wanted was a safe and loving marriage to a man who really loved her. All that any man has to do to provide that safe and loving marriage is listen to the marriage manual in his wife's heart with which God has equipped her.

NO TEN-YEAR-OLD BOY ENVISIONS HIMSELF GROWING UP INTO A CONTROL-FREAK HUSBAND! WE ALL THINK THAT WE WILL BE GREAT HUSBANDS.

Kathy's marriage manual often told me that I was not spending enough time with her. My reaction was to tell her that we were together in the house all day and that she should be happy because most guys had to leave the house to go to work. At least I worked at home and she was with me all day. She would inform me that the dog also was in the house with us! Kathy's marriage manual also told me that I often looked at her in a condescending way. To this I would reply that she was too sensitive and needed to "get a grip".

Your wife is equipped with "red flags" and "warning buzzers". When you do not treat her correctly those red flags will be waving in her heart. When she shares these concerns with you, your first reaction many times will be to resist, deny or argue the point. If you can realize at this point that you are called to love your wife as Christ loved the church and gave his life for her then it will be much easier for you to listen and respond positively to your wife's request.

Kathy's marriage manual "red flags" would really go off when she would make a mistake and I would give her that much-used "put-down look" that was often accompanied by condescending words.

This tactic kept Kathy off balance, causing her to doubt herself, which was my desired outcome as an abusive husband. Her marriage manual would tell me that I was acting like something was wrong with **her** because she made a mistake when it was simply a part of life. This really hurt her feelings. My response was to get defensive and angry, basically telling her to toughen up. Again, I did not have a clue.

It is very simple. When your wife's marriage manual points out that you have violated her in some way, your job is to hear her heart and accept what it is that your personal marriage manual is saying to you. Your wife may not have a clue as how to handle the household checkbook. She may not have a clue as how to run a lawnmower. What she **does** have is that unique marriage manual in her heart for **your** marriage which is given to her from God. The way that a man becomes the man that God has called him to be is to become the husband his wife needs him to be. **The only way to become the husband our wife needs us to be is to read our personal marriage manual.** How do we read that marriage manual? We listen to her heart.

You do not lose when you do this. Everything within you may scream that you are losing yourself. You are losing power. You are losing ground. All of that is a lie of the enemy. **You are becoming the man that God has called you to be by becoming the husband that your wife needs you to be.**

Notice the Bible says that **your prayers** will be hindered if you do not live with **your** wife according to knowledge and **honor** her as the weaker vessel. Honoring your wife is a message that is not often emphasized in popular marriage teachings. Though the message is not heard much, the Bible is clear that we husbands are to honor our wives. Your wife is definitely allowed to remind you of this when you are not meeting her needs! This is fair play!

> **THE ONLY WAY TO BECOME THE HUSBAND OUR WIFE NEEDS US TO BE IS TO READ OUR PERSONAL MARRIAGE MANUAL.**

If you have **any** hope of becoming the man that God has called you to become you will pray that your wife will be bold. In order that your prayers would be answered, your wife must be welcome to tell you when you miss it.

You must provide her a "safe place" emotionally for her to be free to tell you when you don't keep your promises. Your sweetheart must be "allowed" to stand up to you when you are treating her poorly.

If you do not create this freedom in your relationship so that your wife feels free to point out your weaknesses you will not see many answered prayers. You will never become the man that God has called you to become!

For many years, Kathy had **no voice** in our marriage. **She could not talk to me without losing.** I could turn anything around and then spend hours bringing the message home to her as to why her thoughts and feelings were illegitimate. Naturally, only **my** thoughts and feelings were right! Kathy resorted to writing letters to me so that she could bring her thoughts across to me "just right" and without interruption. She would spend up to three days perfecting the letters utilizing the sandwich theory. She would compliment me on what I did right, give me the bad news and end by again telling me something positive.

This tactic did help her cause occasionally. The majority of the time, even these letters did not move me. I really disliked receiving the letters! I would read the masterpiece that she had labored and agonized over. In a huff I would scribble my argumentative replies in the columns and leave the letter for her to find. Sometimes she would change her mind and not even give me a letter that she had prepared. Now those were the letters that I liked!

This is just an example of how desperate a wife can get in trying to communicate to an uncaring and unfeeling husband. The marriage manual in your wife's heart was put there to benefit your marriage. It is a gift to you from

God. It is to be read, heard and heeded! If you do not take your wife's heart seriously, she will explode. That knowledge is inside of her and **she has to do something with it!**

> **IF YOU DO NOT TAKE YOUR WIFE'S HEART SERIOUSLY, SHE WILL EXPLODE.**

Live with **your** wife according to knowledge. All of the knowledge that you need on how to be the husband your wife needs is hidden in her heart, the resting place of your personal marriage manual. Here are some questions borrowed from Life Skills International that you can ask your wife to tap into her built-in marriage manual:

1. Where do we want our relationship to be?

   0 _____ 10

   Worst   Best

2. Where is our relationship in general, today?

   0 _____ 10

   Worst   Best

3. What could we do in the next several days or weeks to bring our relationship closer to where we want it to be?

4. Would spending more time together help?

5. How much time do you feel is needed and what would be the best use of it?

6. What time of day would be a "10" to you for us to spend together?

7. Would more conversation help our relationship?

8. What do you consider meaningful communication?

9. What have I done in the past that might have ruined times of meaningful conversation?

10. How am I doing in the areas of meaningful touch?

11. What could I do to make meaningful touch a "10" for you?

12. How am I doing in my verbal commitments?

13. How can I make our disagreements more of a loving discussion?

14. "What do you need me to do more of to help you grow as a person?"

15. What would be a "10" evening out together if we had a "date night?"

16. What could I do to ruin that "10" evening?

17. What are some ways I could communicate more effectively?

18. What are the ways that I could understand what you go through when you're hurting?

19. What would be a "10" in the way that we make decisions together?

20. What makes you fearful of me?

21. What is the best part of our relationship?

22. What would you change about me if you could?

If you ever hope to become the man that God has called you to be you will have to let your wife know that it is safe for her to share her heart with you. Tone of voice, eye contact, facial expressions, show of interest, sincere desire and patience with the answers are all part of the message you send. You will have to promise that you will not ridicule, belittle or argue with her over the things she shares. If you have been caustic to her needs for years this might take a while. You may have violated her trust so many times that she has closed the marriage manual.

Your job is to convince her that it is safe to try again.

This time you will listen.

GOLDEN KEY

LISTEN TO YOUR WIFE'S HEART!
IT'S YOUR PERSONAL
MARRIAGE MANUAL

GOLDEN KEY

YOU BECOME THE MAN THAT GOD HAS CALLED YOU TO BE

BY BECOMING THE HUSBAND YOUR WIFE NEEDS YOU TO BE

Chapter Eight

He Who Finds
A Wife Finds
A Good Thing

He who **finds a wife** *finds a* **good thing** *and*
obtains favor *from the Lord.*

Proverbs 18:22

By Joel

Kathy is a good thing for me! At one time I was not so sure but time has proven that indeed Kathy is a good thing for me. Because of her I have obtained favor from the Lord.

You might be thinking that your wife does not seem to be a blessing to you and certainly not a route to experiencing the favor of God! Maybe we can change this!

In Proverbs 18:22, "good" is the Hebrew word "towb," one of the twelve Hebrew words for prosperity. It also means "good in its widest sense; beautiful, best, better, cheerful, at ease, prosperous, bountiful, fine, glad, joyful, loving, merry, most pleasant, sweet; favor, pleasure, kindness, goodness, wealth and to be well favored." The promise is that your wife will be good for you! She will be beautiful, the best, cheerful and bountiful. Your wife will bring you favor. She will be joyful, loving, merry, most pleasant and sweet. Your wife will add wealth to your life. Selah. Pause and think calmly about that!

This word "towb" also refers to the glory and the goodness of God! In Exodus 33:19, Moses asked God to let him see His glory. God said that He would make His goodness pass before Moses. The goodness of God is the best part of His Glory! When you found your wife you found the goodness of God in your life, the **best part** of His **Glory!**

You may be wondering why your wife does not seem to be a manifestation of the goodness and glory of God. **Let's discover from the Word how your wife can become a fulfillment of these precious promises in your marriage!**

Psalm 128 says that you are blessed when you fear the Lord and walk in **His** ways. The psalmist identifies one of God's ways as to "eat the labor of your hands." This word labor means "to work and to produce." When you **eat the labor of your hands,** you will get the following results:

1. You will be happy.

2. Your wife will be a fruitful vine in the very heart of your home.

3. It will be well with you.

We are going to isolate the labor of your hands as it applies to the relationship that you have with the wife of your youth. If you could supernaturally see into the foundation of every great marriage you would see a lot of work. At some point in time, these couples who are experiencing great marriages decided to **WORK** on their marriage relationship.

The Bible promises you that if you will **WORK** on your relationship that you will be happy and "it" will be well with you. If you will study on relationships, listen to your wife's heart and work to meet **HER** needs, **YOU** will be happy. **YOU** will reap the benefit. "If momma's happy, everybody's happy! If momma ain't happy, then ain't nobody happy!" The truth is that when you become the husband that your wife needs you to be, **YOU** will be happy! **YOU** will reap the benefit! It will be well with **YOU!**

> **THE TRUTH IS THAT WHEN YOU BECOME THE HUSBAND THAT YOUR WIFE NEEDS YOU TO BE, YOU WILL BE HAPPY, REAP THE BENEFIT AND IT WILL BE WELL WITH YOU.**

What benefits can you anticipate? Your wife will be a fruitful vine in the heart of your home. She will begin to respond to **your** needs. The desire for you that God created within her will leap to life. Her issues will diminish. Your sweetheart will begin to do the things that you have desired. She will start to meet your physical and emotional needs. You will be **her** Knight in shining armor! You will **be her hero! Her man!** She will **want** to do things for you! Suddenly she will be bringing you your coffee! She will begin to brag about you in public!

This is your crowning moment! When your wife is telling everyone what a wonderful husband you are! Her praise is your crown of glory!

Kathy is now everything that I have ever hoped for in a wife. She has fulfilled my fondest imaginations that I pictured in my future as a young man. Kathy is always asking me what she can do for me. Many times I say "nothing really." It is certainly nice that she asks though! When she is working with the kids it is as if she always has her "antenna" up to include me in anything that might bless me.

When I am stressed, Kathy suggests that I sit by myself in a quiet place to read and pray. She asks me if I would like a cup of tea or something to eat. My honey knows that the moment of stress will dissipate and I will emerge from my 30-minute retreat rested and in a good mood. I will enter the room, give her a kiss accompanied by some form of playful and affectionate love touch, squeeze or pat. Kathy is a fruitful vine. Why? I chose to listen to her heart and became the husband that she needed me to be.

Kathy had always worked hard at our relationship but my resistance to the marriage manual in her heart created friction and consternation in our life. When I began to **listen to her heart** she was released to walk in her marital calling of having a desire for her husband.

Kathy's desire for me was now unhindered by my **past** poor treatment of her, disdain for her feelings, put-downs and controlling nature. She became safe because I created a safe place for her. In this safe place, the desire that God placed in her for me came forth.

It is hard for me to describe everything that Kathy is to me, and what she does for me as a teammate, wife, and mom. We work at home. Kathy literally brings breakfast to me just about every morning consisting of fresh carrot juice, vitamins, liquid colloidal minerals and coffee along with something like a muffin, cereal or donut.

If I need something out of the car or from another place in the house and am buried in a project, I only mention it and she normally volunteers immediately to retrieve it. She runs and plays with the kids, home schooled all four of them for nine years and pastors the church with me. We take turns counseling couples in need on the phone, we run Weekend Marriage Intensives and conduct marriage seminars. When funds are low, Kathy offers to run a yard sale. She is always available and almost always interested in love play, anytime, day or night. Speaking of love play, we are constantly touching each other in ways that express our love and interest behind the kids back, as if we are getting away with something! That is a lot of fun!

Fruitful means "to bear fruit and to increase." Your wife will permeate every area of your life. She may not express this in the exact way that Kathy does, but she will manifest this in her own special ways. As you work on your relationship in order to meet your wife's needs, she will be growing like a vine and improving regularly.

If you will work at your marriage, listen to your wife's heart and respond positively to her desires, the Bible promises you three results. First, **you** will be happy! Isn't this what everyone wants in their marriage? Second, your wife will be a fruitful vine who fulfills your fondest dreams!

> **YOUR WIFE WILL BE THE MANIFESTATION OF THE GOODNESS AND GLORY OF GOD IN YOUR LIFE!**

The third result of working on your marriage is that it will be **WELL** with you. The word "**well**" here is the same word with which we opened this chapter, "**towb**".

It will be **well** with you. Your life will be good in its widest sense, beautiful, better, cheerful, prosperous, bountiful, at ease, fine, glad, joyful, loving, merry, most pleasant, pleasurable, sweet, wealthy, full of kindness and well favored.

This is how your life will be if you will work at it and eat the labor of your hands. Proverbs 18:22 states, *"He who finds a wife finds a good thing."* Psalm 128 says that when you receive the fruit from the **labor of your hands,** that it will be well with you. **Your wife will be that good thing that God calls her in Proverbs 18:22!** Your wife will be the manifestation of the goodness and glory of God in your life!

How does your wife become the manifestation of the glory and goodness of God in your life? **Working on your relationship** with her **brings** her into this manifestation of the glory of God! It is a promise from the Bible that you can take to the bank and write checks on! If your wife currently is not a good thing for you then you have not put forth the effort required in your relationship to be the husband that she needs you to be.

When you do, you will say with me, "My wife truly is the goodness and the glory of God manifest in my life." You will be well on the way to becoming the man that God has called you to be. If you will put forth the effort necessary in your relationship with your wife, the Bible promises you that:

1. You will be happy. "When Momma's happy, everybody's happy!"

2. Your wife will permeate every area of your life manifesting the glory and the goodness of God!

3. It will be **well** with **you!**

GOLDEN KEY

YOUR WIFE IS THE GOODNESS OF GOD MANIFEST IN YOUR LIFE

Dear Joel and Kathy,

I have been counseling a married couple for about a month now. There has been some change, but the progress has been slowed by years of disappointment. It has been further complicated by controlling, stubborn temperaments and the husband has only done *some* of his homework. He has shown signs of change, but for only a couple days each week; the rest of the time he reverts to his old behavior. I did not think that I would have any success in getting him to read a whole book on marriage.

When they arrived for their last session, I first met with the husband. After this, he relaxed in the waiting room as I worked with his wife. Imagine my surprise when his wife and I emerged from our session and found him reading "The Man of Her Dreams/The Woman of His!" He said, "I am taking this home. Well, **can** I take this home? I actually am almost done with it." Joel and Kathy, I could hardly believe it! He was 2/3 the way through and couldn't put it down. I was so excited to see him fully interested in his marriage in that way.

THREE WEEKS LATER…

Joel and Kathy, the couple I wrote about is doing great. He is making a strong commitment to his wife and really working on meeting her needs. Your book has been a great help with this couple and has added a new dimension to our counseling. I was seeing movement, but after the book I really saw excitement.

I am very pleased at the approach you take in this book. You are real people with real answers. I have ordered additional copies for use with clients and I highly recommend its use to other professional marriage counselors. Praise God!

Lisa Winchell
Licensed Pastoral Counselor

Chapter Nine

That Time Of Month... Man's Best Friend!

*Husbands, love your wives as Christ also loved the church **and gave Himself for her.***
Ephesians 5:25

Agree with your adversary quickly!
Matthew 5:25

By Joel

Your wife is not your adversary! Your wife is your lover and best friend. Confused and surprised by our amazing insight, husbands often exclaim to us that their wives say these exact words to them all the time! If a husband is full of pride and responding out of insecurity though, he may **create** an adversary out of his wife!

When you listen to the marriage manual in your wife's heart you will appreciate it when she opens up and talks to you about what you are doing that is hurting her or your relationship. This is a key to your growth as a man of God.

"Thanks For Pointing That Out!"

Here is a simple key to success. When your wife points out an area in your life that needs changing, the correct response is "Thanks for pointing that out!"

You have **no idea** how the things you are doing or saying, or not doing or saying, are affecting your wife. Gary Smalley points out that women are like butterflies, men are like bulls!

When the wind blows, a butterfly is blown about and carried wherever it goes. It is sensitive and responsive to the slightest breeze. A hard wind will knock the butterfly to the ground and break its wings. It will lie on the ground, helpless until it breathes its last. This happens from a simple gust of wind!

> **"OK, SORRY ABOUT THAT. I DID NOT REALIZE THAT I AM COMING ACROSS LIKE I AM YELLING. TELL ME HOW YOU NEED ME TO TALK TO YOU ABOUT THIS."**

The bull on the other hand would not have even noticed that the wind was blowing. For that matter, it would not even notice if it stepped on the gasping butterfly as it struggles for survival.

When your wife says to you, "Quit yelling at me," you do **not** respond with, "I am not yelling… I am just talking to you." Your reply should be, "OK, sorry about that. I did not realize that I am coming across like I am yelling. Tell me how you need me to talk to you about this."

If your wife says to you, "We never do anything fun," don't reply by saying, "Yes we do, we just went out to eat last month. What do you **call that?"**

The correct reply is to say, "Oh, I did not realize that we were lacking in having fun. You know how busy I get with daily affairs. Thanks for bringing this up. What would be some things that you can think of that we can do together to have fun?"

Pick one! Do it! Take a bike ride, play tennis, go to a movie. Do something that **she** wants to do which represents fun to **her.**

Like that butterfly, your wife can sense when the wind shifts in your relationship. She is affected by the slightest change in the breeze. The bull responds to her concerns that something is wrong like, "Duh, what are you talkin' about? I don't feel nothin'. Everything is fine. Chill woman!" If she is truly reeling and making a scene, the bull thinks that the best approach is to just step on her to put her out of her misery!

Recently Tom told his wife Sandy that all of the things she wanted to do were "dumb" and "worthless". He did not like to compete so her idea of playing tennis was a dumb idea. His idea of fun would be to take a hike, go to a fair or go camping.

I pointed out that all of Tom's ideas were large projects that would require much pre-planning due to their young children and their work schedules. These were all eight to twelve hour fun ideas.

Sandy, on the other hand, suggested tennis. They could go to the free tennis courts 10 minutes from home, play for 30 minutes and be home within an hour.

Tom's reply was to say that he was not interested in playing tennis! This is not about Tom. This is about **Sandy** and doing what **Sandy** wants to do. It is not all about Tom!

We men can be very "thick" sometimes!

It really comes down to pride and ego. We have to be dead to ourselves to not respond out of pride. We have to love our wives as Christ loved the church and gave Himself for us.

Husbands are many times so full of insecurity that they respond in pride when their wives try to tell them **anything** about how to be the husbands that they need them to be.

"OK. Thanks for pointing that out." These are "magic words" which will give you a marriage relationship that will improve drastically in a short time.

I wish you would clean up after yourself.
Oh. OK. Thanks for pointing that out. I will get right on it.

I wish you would tell me that you love me more often.
Oh. OK. Thanks for reminding me. I love you, sweetheart, and I will try to tell you more often.

You never bring me flowers.
You are right. It has been a long time since I have brought you flowers. I hate to admit that I have forgotten

all about that, so thanks for reminding me. You can count on getting some flowers soon.

Lately, you have been spending more time with your friends (clients, church members, etc.) than you spend with me.

Oh my, you are right. I have been feeling that same way myself, sorry about that. Let's get a sitter tonight and go out on a date for just the two of us.

I am concerned about you. It does not seem like you have been spending any time in the Word and prayer lately.

Ouch. That hurts. But you are right and I appreciate you noticing and saying something about it. That helps me a lot to have you helping me to be accountable. I have been so buried lately. Thanks for pointing that out. I am going to go sit down with the Word right now. Would you fix us some tea and join me?

This is easy if you are dead to yourself. When full of pride and insecurity it is almost impossible to respond in this life-giving manner. This is the only way to become the Man that God has called you to be; by becoming the husband your wife needs you to be. There are no shortcuts.

You become the *man* that *God* has called you to be by becoming the *husband* that your *wife needs* you to be.

Do you remember the verse from the beginning of chapter seven?

Likewise, ye husbands, **dwell with them according to knowledge, giving honor unto the wife as unto the weaker vessel** *and as being heirs together of the grace of life,* **that your prayers be not hindered.**

1 Peter 3:7

Your aim is to read the marriage manual that is in your wife's heart. This is the means by which you can discover things you can **do** to **be the man of your wife's dreams** and things you can **eliminate** that **hurt** your relationship.

> **PMS STANDS FOR "PACK MY SUITCASE!" ALL I WANT TO DO IS GET OUT OF HERE WHEN IT IS THAT TIME OF THE MONTH!**

Your biggest challenge is to get her to open up and talk to you honestly about what you can do differently to improve your relationship.

God has given us a gift that will aid us in our efforts! This gift is designed to help us hear our wife's heart concerning things that might be bothering her. If all else fails, your wife's marriage manual will definitely open once a month!

This is why we say that **your wife's monthly is your best friend!**

"What's that? That time of month is man's best friend! **You have got to be kidding me!** PMS stands for 'Pack my suitcase!' All that I want to do is **get out of here** when it is that time of month!"

At one time, I felt the same way. I was convinced that the only reason Kathy would get upset when that time came was because **she** had a problem with which **she** had to deal. This problem had nothing to do with **me** as far as I was concerned. I "felt badly for her" that she would get so **touchy and uptight** but what **really** upset me was that she would **point out things that had been secretly bothering her all month!**

When she would start down this road I would argue with her, "This has not bothered you **all month** and now, **just because you are on your monthly,** it's a problem! This is not fair. Just get over it. In three days it won't bother you anymore."

Sure enough, when three days went by the issue would get safely tucked back under the rug. Many times the same issue would suddenly "re-appear" like clockwork... month after month after month. My response was to make a few half-hearted attempts at satisfying her "demand" and then "fluff it off" as soon as the eruption subsided.

What is really going on when this happens? It is very simple. Your wife wants a good relationship with you. She is **desperate** for a **happy** marriage.

All month long your sweetheart puts up with the little, inconsiderate things that you do: the mean looks, the harsh words, the put down sounds. On top of this she has to beg you to do your fair share around the house. I can hear you argue with her, "I work all day, I should not have to help around the house."

All month long, your wife puts up with these childish, immature postures in relationship to your responsibilities as a husband and father.

Suddenly, like a Mack truck, the dreaded monthly hits. Now, your wife's defenses are not as strong. Suddenly, when you hurt her feelings she cannot overlook it as she has done all month.

Suddenly, when you refuse to lend an ear she feels rejected and lashes out at you. The fact that you **bowl** with the **guys** twice a week and only spend **30 minutes** of quality time with **her** has also **suddenly** become an issue.

> **SUDDENLY, LIKE A MACK TRUCK, THE DREADED MONTHLY HITS.**

This is it! This is your Best Friend! Why? Because **suddenly** you get a chance to discover areas in which you have to grow!

Suddenly you become painfully aware that you have been acting like an adult child all month and not meeting your wife's needs!

The adult child responds to his wife's every mood, positive **or** negative. When she gets negative he gets even more negative and the situation escalates. This is why these male children cry in unison,

"She **made** me angry."

"If only **my wife** would get **off** my **case** I would **treat** her better."

"She **made** me hit her."

Mature men do not **respond** to their wife's negativity; mature men **initiate** actions or words of love and kindness to meet their wife's need.

This brings security and healing.

He grows up emotionally and the dreaded monthly loses all of its power. Her needs are met. He is maturing. Everyone is more peaceful and the relationship is satisfying and fulfilling. The marriage is beginning to look like a marriage made in heaven.

Kathy and I have not had a bad "time of month" together in years! Previous to 1994, they were a living nightmare!

Thank God for this gift! If it were not for "that time of month," you might have gone on living like a child for the remainder of your married life!

GOLDEN KEY

THANK GOD FOR YOUR WIFE'S MONTHLY: MAN'S BEST FRIEND!

Something to Think About

THE DEFINITION OF INSANITY
(A word to the soon-to-be-wise…)

Insanity is continuing to do the exact same thing that you have always done, yet expecting different results *this* time!

Why does one man demand to know what his wife is thinking when she does not want to tell him? This man continues to push on her until a huge argument results. He never realizes that she just wants some space. He wants her to respond to him and gets angry that she wants space. To this man, the fact that she does not want to talk about what is bothering her is an attack on his ego. How can she dare to want some private time in her thought life?

Another man does not ask his wife what is wrong and his wife is offended that he does not ask. He figures that if she wants to tell him what is wrong, she has a tongue and could do so if she wanted. He is actually quite glad that she is clammed up. To him, this is peace. Because he does not ask what she is thinking, a huge argument ensues.

This does not mean that women are impossible to understand. This does not mean that these two couples should swap partners.

It simply is further proof that God gives every man a wife who has the perfect needs for him to fulfill. In order to meet her need, he has to die to himself and the way that he thinks that he should relate to his wife.

The clueless husband simply continues the same approach to his wife, with disastrous results. He thinks, that perhaps *this* time, he will get a different result.

Husbands, live with *your* wife with understanding. 1 Peter 3:7a

Chapter Ten

Why Make
The Effort?

He who is **married cares** *about* **how he may please his wife. She** *who is* **married cares** *about* **how she may please her husband.**
1 Corinthians 7:33-34 *(condensed)*

By Kathy

Is this really worth the effort? Many people throw in the towel and find another spouse! Why should we work to have a dream marriage with our currently "flawed" spouse? Why strive to again fall in love with this spouse who has a history of problems when we can simply get divorced and find a better one? I was determined that our children would grow up with two happy and successful parents in an intact home. This would illustrate to them that they could be loving mates for their future spouses. If children do not witness their parents showing affection to one another by hugging, kissing and other acts of appreciation they will grow up without an example of an affectionate marriage.

Randy and Charlotte explained that there had not been much affection shown in either of their families. They were now perpetuating this cycle of not expressing affection to one another or to their children. They were actually sleeping in separate bedrooms! Their children are learning from them that this is marriage: sleeping in separate bedrooms with little display of affection in public or in private! Sam and Stacy were sitting on their couch holding hands. **Their** 8-year-old daughter came down the stairs and stared at them. After a long moment she happily turned and went on her merry way. The message that was received by **this** impressionable 8-year-old from mom and dad was, "All is well on the home front. Your world is safe and secure. We are not going anywhere." In this day of instant marriage and divorce our children **must know that their home is safe.** It is a place where they can sleep well and play freely, a place where they know mom and dad love and care for each other deeply. This is security!

> ALL IS WELL ON THE HOME FRONT. YOUR WORLD IS SAFE AND SECURE. WE ARE NOT GOING ANYWHERE.

"Children are resilient." This statement was created to excuse selfish people who are determined to "do their own thing". It is a clever phrase enabling them to live in denial over the long-term pain "their thing" causes. There **are** long-term consequences that carry on into the adult lives of children who are raised in a dysfunctional family. Joel's parents divorced when he was ten years old. If you met Joel today you would meet a well-adjusted family man who loves the Lord and is completely in love with his wife and children. He supports his family well financially, emotionally and spiritually. Truly Joel could be a poster child for the propaganda that portrays children of divorce recovering successfully. What did Joel go through on the way here, though? He began smoking marijuana at **ten years old**, which "coincidentally" was the same year his parents were divorced. At 13, Joel was **selling** marijuana and had graduated to personally using "speed" and "downers". By the time he reached 15, he was using LSD. That same year he was convicted of theft and sentenced to spend six months in a juvenile delinquent ranch. Joel was finally born again at 17 years of age while doing time in solitary confinement for aiding and abetting in an armed robbery!

Eight years later we were married and pastoring our first church. At 29 years of age, Joel repeated history by committing adultery in the same way his dad did. The rest is history. Recently we have discovered that a nervous habit that has plagued Joel since childhood is linked directly to his parents' divorce some 33 years ago! Healing of this habit is a current prayer project for us! Think about that! It has **been over 30 years** and Joel is **still** being affected! According to secular thought he is resilient.

Those who believe that children are resilient and recover easily from divorce must believe that if the children do not become mass murderers or commit suicide that their point has been proven! Work it out. Now! The bottom line of a re-marriage is that a divorced woman is going to marry yet another man who will not be prepared to meet her needs. He will need to learn and he will also resist said learning. A divorced man will marry a woman who (God-forbid!) also has needs – and he again will find that he does not want to meet them. It is much easier to get your current marriage to be a success rather than starting over in a new one. We understand that if a spouse is unwilling to participate in creating a happy marriage, you are left with no choice, but let your battle cry be "Never say die!" until it is absolutely crystal clear that their will be no change.

Now, while we emphasize so strongly the importance of families staying together, we need to be perfectly clear about physically abusive relationships. We will **never** recommend that a woman stay in a **physically** abusive relationship. A woman in this situation needs help to find a way of escape for her children and herself. Staying would be the worst of two evils and affect her children more deeply than divorce. A woman who is subjected to physical abuse has a responsibility to teach her children that physical abuse is not acceptable.

> **THOSE WHO BELIEVE THAT CHILDREN RECOVER EASILY FROM DIVORCE MUST BELIEVE THAT THEIR POINT IS PROVEN IF THE CHILDREN DON'T BECOME MASS MURDERERS.**

There is a procedure of escape and counseling outlined by Life Skills that can be followed in hopes of seeing the family restored. When a woman escapes an abusive situation, the abuser will normally go through a cycle of response. They will respond first in rage followed by a grand show of repentance. There will be tears, pleas for restoration, promises to change and expressions of love. A woman cannot fall for this or she will soon find that she is being beaten again. When the abuser realizes that she is not going to let him come back he will fly into a rage again.

This second rage can be a scary time and if the family is not in hiding, a restraining order needs to be filed with the police along with a request for police surveillance. When the second rage has run its course, it will again be replaced by a sullen, repentant, pleading, broken man who is promising to change forever. Flowers, gifts, money — **nothing** is too extravagant in this second attempt to display that he is a changed man. You again cannot fall for this. There **will be** a third period of rage after this rejection.

If the wife has held her ground through all three periods of rage and the abuser **comes to the place of repentance for a third time** he is then ready to enter into serious individual counseling. He has the potential to be 100% changed. Note that I did **not** say that it was time for her to let him come back home. If the counselor is successful at getting the abuser to accept responsibility for his actions and quit blaming his wife for the abuse then an extended period of mutual counseling can begin with the hope of seeing the marriage restored.

For further help with escape from a serious physically abusive relationship, contact Life Skills International using the contact information included in the preface. There are Life Skills Centers across the U.S. that can either help you or direct you to other helpful agencies in your area.

There are no gray areas when it comes to physical abuse. When the abuse is mental, emotional, verbal or spiritual, there are a variety of options that a wife may consider. Asking her husband to leave the home until he completes reading this book and makes changes is one of those options. Other options include seeking counseling, attending a Weekend Marriage Intensive and speaking up in defense of herself and not allowing the abuse to continue. Living under further abuse is not an option. Things must change. That is why this book is in your hands. This is not a coincidence. This is a God-thing.

We were very successful living the principles of successful married life that we had learned through Life Skills during our second pastorate.

It was during our **first** pastorate that we were having difficulties in our marriage. I still remember clearly the encounter that we had in the parking lot after church one evening. "Joel, I really need your help. I am getting overwhelmed with the ministry, counseling people, witnessing, the children, (1½ years old and six months respectively) and the house. I need you to help me with more things around the house." Joel's reply was to tell me that I could choose which way it was going to be. Either **he** could run the **house** and **I** run the church or **he** would run the church and **I** would run the household. There was no cooperation, no help; there was no give and take.

Our second year of marriage was especially difficult. One incident I remember clearly was when Joel announced that he was going to be gone for the evening to watch two movies at the local theatre. I asked him to watch one and come home to spend some time with me. I promised to make a cake and we planned to play a card game, something I enjoyed at the time.

At the end of the first movie, Joel blew into the house. In his rush he did not see the cake that I had made. Joel yelled on his way **back** out the door, "You lied to me! You told me that you would be waiting for me when I got back and would have a cake ready. You are just trying to control me. You tricked me to get me not to go to the second movie."

There was no time for me to point out to him that the cake was made. Later I explained to Joel that the cake had indeed been ready and how disappointed I was. Joel lightly apologized. Of course! It was easy **after** the deed was done! He had gotten his way at my expense and could "slough" it all off with a simple apology.

We are bearing our hearts to give you hope that any marriage can be healed regardless of the severity or specifics of your particular situation. If our marriage was healed, yours can be healed, too. He can become the man of your dreams and you can become the woman of his! Whatever your issues are, whatever your pain is, whatever your past is, take it from us – a successful marriage with your current spouse is definitely worth the effort! Yes! It works! Lives **can** be **changed!** Regardless of the past you **can** have a **dream marriage.**

GOLDEN KEY

A DREAM MARRIAGE
IS ALWAYS WORTH THE EFFORT

Dear Kathy and Joel,
What a difficult thing to accomplish – becoming one!! What a simple but awesome concept designed to achieve that!! When Charles and Frances Hunter gave us your book, I picked it up and was riveted! I literally did not put it down until I had read it all! I could not believe how awesomely simple and 'right on' it is. The next night I read it a second time! "The Man of Her Dreams/The Woman of His!" has changed my life!

What an empowering revelation to hear that I have the right to expect a deep, meaningful, bonded, and successful relationship with my husband in which my needs are valued and met!!

What a relief to know that I'm not a lunatic after all! That is how I used to feel when I responded negatively to being ignored, feeling devalued and unloved!! What a liberating validation knowing that I have a right to expect to be an equal member of the marital team!! Thank you, Kathy and Joel, for writing this book that has so empowered me!! I wish every couple – married or about to be – would have a copy of this awesome book!!

Linda, Former Mayor, A small town in Texas

Dear Joel and Kathy,
Thank you for all the "real world" advice. From your insights I have learned to better appreciate my wife's feelings and perspective. Many helpful ideas and principles are presented in a very clear and useful manner. I recommend "The Man of Her Dreams/The Woman of His!" to all couples. It is very insightful and makes it easy to understand that continued communication is key to a healthy relationship.

Wallace, A small town in Texas

Chapter Eleven

Leading As
A Team

So that servant came, and shewed his lord these things. Then the **master of the house** *said to his servant.*

Luke 14:21

By Joel

Kathy and I have discovered through study of the Word that God desires the husband and wife to lead the home **together** as a **team.** This eliminates the opportunity for the husband to use spiritually abusive phrases such as, "You have to submit to me" and "I am the head of this house."

If God requires that the husband and wife lead the house **together** as a **team,** giving them both the **same job description,** then **teamwork** is required. Communication is required. **A meeting of the hearts and minds** is required.

One time, Kathy and I considered moving to Texas. I felt like all of my ministry dreams would come true if we could be a part of a particular large ministry located in Dallas at the time. My plan was to serve the pastor, with my goal being that he would raise me up into ministry. Kathy felt very strongly against it.

Even though this was early in my marriage and I was in my control-freak glory, I had enough sense to heed that really strong warning my wife sensed in her spirit. It was not long after this that the ministry in Texas fell into a bad season and closed its doors. The move to Dallas would have been a disaster. When the ministry closed, I realized how right Kathy was and I began to get a glimmer that **maybe** the man is not **supposed** to be the **"end all"** in leading the home.

If there **is** a decision that **absolutely must be made immediately** and there is no agreement, it falls on someone to make that final decision. However, this virtually **should never happen.** I cannot **imagine** a decision that could not be postponed until the husband and wife are able to reach an **agreement or compromise** that leaves both parties satisfied. How did Kathy and I look at this after Life Skills? I asked her, "Kathy, I buy into all of this, but if there is a decision that must be made and we simply cannot agree and it is d-day, do you mind if I still get to make that final decision?" She said, "Sure." In 14 years, this has never happened. 14 years later, I realize that was my immaturity and insecurity speaking. The man getting the "final decision" privilege is cultural. It is not a New Testament concept. We work as a team. We don't even consider this question anymore.

How does this work in the myriad of decisions that must be made on a daily basis? Kathy and I find many times that one of us feels strongly about something and the other one does not really care about the particular issue. In this case there is no debate. We go with the one who feels strongly about the situation.

When I was a control-freak the direction **always** had to originate with me. If Kathy felt strongly about something, it was **all the more** reason for me to pull rank and inform her that **I** was the head of the house and we were going to do it **my** way.

> **I CANNOT IMAGINE A DECISION THAT COULD NOT BE POSTPONED UNTIL THE HUSBAND AND WIFE ARE ABLE TO REACH AN AGREEMENT OR COMPROMISE THAT LEAVES BOTH PARTIES SATISFIED.**

This is the summary of an argument between Kathy and me in 1986: "Can we go out to dinner Friday night?" "No." "Why not? We normally go out to eat dinner about once a week and it has been a few weeks." "I am the one who picks the nights we go out." "Well that is not fair. I feel like we have not had any quality time and that we need to go out this Friday."

"Would you please drop the subject? I am the head of this house and I will decide when we go out to eat. When it is time, I will tell you. Until then, just leave me alone."

This upset Kathy for a few days until she successfully "swallowed it", reminding herself that she had to "submit in all things except for sin." "Submit in all things except for sin," was the message taught by the then very popular, and now recently divorced "Father of Marriage Ministry" who was an influence in our life at the time. We had been to his seminar in person, purchased and studied the complete 16 tape series with study guide and attempted to assimilate the information. We definitely embraced the submission emphasis of the teachings!

Kathy's brother was visiting our home at the time and she vented to him. Not knowing what to say, he gave her his best input saying that many men did not take their wives out to dinner at all and that she might as well be happy that we at least do go out together occasionally. This was helpful and heartfelt advice at the time. He did not have a copy of *The Man of Her Dreams/The Woman of His!* to give to Kathy so the very popular "submit to keep the peace" message was the best that he or anyone could offer!

One time when I came home, Kathy had the radio on very loud. She was enjoying listening to Christian music while "bee-bopping" around the house cleaning, vacuuming and having a happy moment. I turned her music off and put a tape in that I wanted to listen to without considering her.

"Oh. Hi Joel. Welcome home. By the way, I was listening to that music while I was cleaning the house and really enjoying it. Will you put it back on for me?"

All that Kathy was asking for was a little respect and consideration, which was a very reasonable request! Yes, it is reasonable to a man who does not feel that he is being threatened if he is not always in control.

A huge argument ensued in which I again informed Kathy that I was the "king of the castle" and that we would listen to what I wanted to listen to if there was a question. The argument ended with me telling Kathy to get onto her knees. I held her hands up while leading her in a prayer of repentance for her bad attitude, rebellion and lack of submission.

You may wonder what goes on in the head of a control-freak in these situations. Why would he/she demand that every decision, every activity, every thought go their way? A highly developed combination of pride and insecurity causes a person to manifest this level of knee-jerk control. They feel like they are losing some sense of self-worth if they "give in" to their partner.

Randy would allow his wife to come up with her own ideas and then complain, "Why is she going to the store? We were just there yesterday. Look at how long she is gone. If she just went to the store she would have been home by now. I called her and it did not sound to me like she was at the store. I did not hear any background noise. If she were at the store I would have heard background noise." When she arrives home Randy demands accountability for her every minute. He often checks the car odometer and cell phone records to verify that she did not go anywhere else or make unexplained phone calls.

We are not making this up. Every story that we relate in this book is true. Yes, names and locations have been changed but they are all true case examples from our life or from marriages of other believers with whom we are personally familiar.

Perhaps you believe that this is not common in Christian homes. The truth is that control and manipulation are **very** common among our ranks. It is compounded by the fact that manipulative and controlling men always want to point to other men who have the same problem and say, "I am not as bad as him."

We realize that the open sharing of our life will tempt some men to use our worst case examples as an "out" in order to avoid accepting responsibility for their own issues. Do not do this. You will not grow.

Bill told his wife, "I did not commit adultery like Joel did, so this does not apply to me." Is that right? Is this your attitude? Jesus claimed that when you look on a woman to lust, that you have committed adultery with her. Are you saying that you have never looked on a woman in lust since the day you were married? Perhaps we should discuss your tendency toward lying. Perhaps you simply disagree with Jesus. Your lusting is not really adultery. Oh. You disagree with Jesus? The altars are open as we sing three refrains of "Just as I Am."

Paul Hegstrom was much worse than I was. He was faced with attempted murder charges from almost killing a girlfriend while separated from Judy. When he was with Judy, his wife, he would leave her in a pool of blood from his abusive tirades. When he spoke, I listened.

If the principles that Paul was teaching were his answers, then perhaps they were also mine. I resisted, but Paul pried my mind open (with a verbal crow bar) and confronted me with the truth. It never crossed my mind to dodge that truth by saying, "Well, at least I am not as bad as Paul. These principles worked for **him**. He needed **serious** help, but I don't beat Kathy." I did try to dodge by claiming that our troubles were all Kathy's fault, but Paul would not let me get away with it.

If you are squirming, desperately clinging to excuses as to why the things we are teaching do not apply to you, do yourself a favor and give it up. They apply to you. You need to learn how to lay your life down for your wife. You need to learn how to function with your wife as a team. You need to value her as your God-given equal. Your partner. Your teammate. Learn it. Live it. Love it.

As we stated in the beginning of this book, our marriage issues had nothing to do with the adultery. Our issues were alive and well for the 7 years leading up to the affair. The adultery was no more than a wake up call for us that our issues were much deeper than my acting on an attraction to another woman. We had serious issues and did not have a clue how to repair them.

You may not have ever committed adultery like I did. You may not beat your wife as Paul did. However, you have not been everything that you are called by God to be in your marriage. That much everyone knows; especially your wife and her best friends, who are sworn to silence.

Don't wait for a more serious wake up call. With the millions of books in print on planet earth, let the fact that this book miraculously made it into your hands be your wake up call. You are reading these words right now.

What is that I hear? Is that the still, small voice of God speaking? Hello! It is a new day. You can become the man that God has called you to be by becoming the husband that your wife needs you to be. This is no accident. This is not coincidence. This is destiny.

Perhaps you have not committed adultery, nor have you physically beaten your wife. Your wife has suffered at your hands in other ways than Kathy suffered at mine. Your wife has needs that Kathy may not have had. In order for you to grow into the man that God has called you to be you must meet the needs that **your** wife expresses. Live with **your wife** according to knowledge.

The needs that **your** wife has are specific and unique to **her.** They are custom designed, by God, to challenge **your** pride and insecurities. When you learn to meet **your wife's specific needs** then you are growing into the man that God has called you to be! Yes, you could read every marriage book and custom design the ultimate "wife-satisfying plan". But, guess what? The plan that you design would not work on your wife!

> THE NEEDS THAT YOUR WIFE HAS ARE SPECIFIC AND UNIQUE TO HER. THEY ARE CUSTOM MADE FOR YOUR MARRIAGE.

Why is this? God is requiring you to listen to and bond with **your** wife. You don't bond when you are in control. You don't bond by creating "the ultimate plan" to meet "every" woman's needs. You bond when you listen to **your** wife's heart – and meet **your** wife's needs.

We give your wife permission to say to you, "You may not have treated me as poorly as Joel treated Kathy but you have your issues. You are also controlling and manipulative in your relationship to me." We give you, man of God who is reading this book, permission to grow into the **man** that **God** has called you to be by welcoming her input.

Let's look closer at this idea of leading the home. The first word we will look at is the word "proistemi" *(4291 in Strong's)*, which means "to stand before in rank, to preside or to be over." It is used in Romans 12 when discussing the motivational gifts.

> *He that ruleth, with diligence;*
>
> *Romans 12:8*

The word for ruling here **is not referring only to men** even though it says, "he that ruleth". All of the other motivational gifts of the Spirit listed in Romans would then also have to be reserved exclusively for men such as the gifts of mercy, giving, teaching or exhortation.

As you well know, if we left it up to the men to show all of the mercy, do all of the giving, teaching, exhorting and leading in our churches then not very much would get done! The same word is used when referring to elders ruling in the church.

> *Let the elders that **rule well** be counted worthy of double honor, especially they who labor in the word and doctrine.*
>
> *1 Timothy 5:17*

Let's see how this word is used when exclusively applying to men. When referring to leading the family, Paul says,

> *One that* **ruleth well his own house**...
> *having his children in subjection. (For if a man*
> *know not how to* **rule his own house***, how*
> *shall he take care of the church of God?)*
> *1 Timothy 3:4a, 5*

> *Let the deacons be the husbands of one wife,*
> **ruling** *their children and* **their own houses**
> **well***.*
> *1 Timothy 3:12*

Men who tend toward being spiritually abusive will remind their wives almost daily that as husbands they are supposed to rule the house. His idea of ruling is to be controlling and manipulative, always wanting to get his way, ruling with an iron fist, raising his voice if anyone disagrees with him and demanding loyalty to his every whim and desire.

How would you like it if this were how the pastors and elders ruled in church! The same word applies in both circumstances! Wouldn't you rather have your church elders being servant-leaders? The same measure you measure out will be measured back to you!

These verses show very clearly that men are to lead the house. Before you get too haughty though, let's take a look at some Bible references that clearly specify that **women** are **also** authorized to **lead the house.**

Therefore I desire that the younger widows marry, bear children, **manage the house,** *give no opportunity to the adversary to speak reproachfully.*
1 Timothy 5:14

The word translated here as "manage" the house, means to be the **head of a family!** The Greek word is **"oikodespoteo"** *(3616 in Strong's)* which means, "to be the head of" or in other words "**to rule**" a family.

> **THE WORD TRANSLATED AS "MANAGE" THE HOUSE MEANS TO BE THE HEAD OF A FAMILY!**

Now it is getting hot in here.

The King James Version interprets this as to "guide the house". That was a safe translation.

I can imagine that if the translators had translated the word **literally** that women are to be the **head of a family** or **rule the family** there would have been problems. They might have heard the much feared words from the king, "Off with his head!"

The word we just looked at, **"oikodespoteo,"** is taken from the word **"oikodespotes,"** which means exactly the same thing: to be the head of a family. King James translates this in other verses as "goodman of the house", "householder" and "master of the house."

For the kingdom of heaven is like unto a man that is an **householder,** *which went out early in the morning to* **hire laborers into his vineyard.**
Matthew 20:1

The word used in Matthew 20:1 to describe a wife's leadership in the home is "householder". This person was **in charge!** He hired the laborers. This is a parable describing leadership in the same way that a wife is authorized to be the head of the house.

> *So that servant came, and shewed his lord these things. Then the **master of the house** being angry said to his servant, Go out quickly into the streets and lanes of the city, and bring in hither the poor, and the maimed, and the halt, and the blind.*
>
> *Luke 14:21*

> **WE ARE AFTER TEAMWORK AND MUTUAL RESPECT WHEN IT COMES TO LEADING THE FAMILY UNIT.**

Here the word is translated "master of the house". This is what the wife is supposed to be! The master of the house! How can this be? **How can God tell both the husband and wife to be the head of the house together?**

HE IS GOD! God planned it this way! God's plan for leadership in your home is one of team leadership and mutual submission. Another word to describe mutual submission would be mutual "adaptation".

What are we after? We are after teamwork and mutual respect when it comes to leading the family unit. That is what the Bible teaches; husbands and wives working together, leading their home as a team. The two become ONE!

You can do this. I know it is a new paradigm. Just remember that the goal is to grow up.

Adults do not always demand their way. Toddlers do. You really do not want to stay at the emotional age of a toddler.

Emphasizing that you are the head of the house and demanding that your wife submit to and obey you only does one thing. It leaves you as a forty- or fifty-year-old toddler who throws temper tantrums when things do not go his way.

Quit living like this. You are better than that.

The only way for you to become the man that God has called you to be is to become the husband your wife needs you to be.

GOLDEN KEY

DECIDE TO LEAD YOUR HOME AS A TEAM

Dear Joel and Kathy,

"The Man of Her Dreams/The Woman of His!" should be mandatory reading for every married couple in ministry. There are a lot of couples in ministry that never would have experienced the heartbreak of divorce if they could have got hold of the wisdom this book shares.

Thank you so much for your continued help and encouragement at such a difficult time in my life.

Margarita, Church Co-Founder, Florida

Hi Joel and Kathy!

Tina and I are doing great!

It is amazing how much progress we've made in our marriage in the past few months after 15 years of dysfunction.

I gave the book to my father (my dad and I are much alike). He is now working the program and attending our men's support group with Tom and Jim.

Your book is really changing lives!

Tina and I look forward to seeing you again in April. Keep up the good work!

Adam & Tina Smith

Chapter Twelve

Your Wife Ain't Your Momma!
(And You Are NOT Her Old Man!)

By Joel

In the last chapter, we discovered that God has authorized wives as well as their husbands to lead the home as a team in unity and harmony. Titus 2:5 talks about wives being "keepers at home." This is the Greek word "oikourgos", meaning "to be a guard, domestically inclined and a good housekeeper." Husbands like this one! However, as we are learning, we always act as a team.

We have four children. I pitch in around our house by doing laundry and anything else Kathy asks me to do. One thing that I do is wipe down the commodes when I notice they need it. I am especially good at reminding the kids to do their chores! This actually helps, as sometimes Kathy gets so wrapped up in her business that the kids get away with "forgetting" until I remind them!

Helping around the house is an easy way for you to lighten the load. Your wife is not your "momma". Pick up your dirty socks and underwear! Hopefully your momma taught you to clean your room and you continued the habit after you were married! If you were a slob as a single man or if your momma **did** pick up after you, that changes now!

Your wife ain't your momma **or** your personal housekeeper! She is your lover and your best friend! Help around the house! Hire a housecleaner! Do something. Do anything! As long as you are lightening the load off of your wife's back, you are doing a good thing.

Be careful in how you verbally refer to one another. Your wife is not your "Momma," "Mom," "Mother" or "Old Lady". These are not terms that magnify your status as lovers, friends and teammates. At the same time, you are not your wife's father. You are not her old man or her dad. These terms do not magnify your status as lovers and friends.

Call each other anything else that **magnifies the relationship that you want to have.** Call one another honey, sweetheart, beautiful, sexy, gorgeous, man of God, woman of God and any other pet names that you personally like. These are great and they build momentum towards a God-based love relationship.

Comparable

And the Lord God said, "It is not good that man Should be alone; I will make him a helper ***comparable*** *to him."*
Genesis 2:18

When you married, you did not marry up or down. This may come as a surprise, as in many marriages one of the partners invariably feels like they married "below his or her level". This is simply not so. A man's wife is comparable to her husband. Two $1,000 bills are comparable, **period**. One is not better than the other!

In the beginning of our marriage I felt as though I were superior to Kathy. When I began to grow into the man God called me to be by becoming the husband my wife needed me to be, things started to look different. I realized how incredible Kathy was. I began to realize how strong she had been to survive the bad years. I realized what a wonderful wife and lover she was. She was my equal in every way!

This was a revolution in my marriage. I did not marry down; therefore I could not **look down** on Kathy.

> **A MAN'S WIFE IS COMPARABLE TO HER HUSBAND. TWO $1,000 BILLS ARE COMPARABLE, PERIOD. ONE IS NOT BETTER THAN THE OTHER.**

My 'looking down' on Kathy had simply been a pride- and ego-protecting mechanism common to abusive men.

I married at my exact level. If I looked down on Kathy I had to realize that I had faults that were equal hers.

This realization pulled the rug out from under me.

I used to assign errands to Kathy as if I was her dad. I would send her out the door knowing that if she did anything wrong or incomplete I would use her mistake as an opportunity to insult her, belittle her, put her down or just give her one of "those looks" that translated into, "How can you be such an idiot?" I always found something that she did incorrectly or incompletely.

It did not matter how good of a job she had done at accomplishing my detailed assignment. For some insane reason I wanted Kathy to realize how inept she was! I got some kind of bizarre satisfaction out of trying to make her feel inadequate.

I now know that it was because I was afraid of losing her. By making her feel inadequate I thought that I could keep her under my thumb. By tarnishing her self-image I could make her "feel" like she was fortunate to be married to me. If she lost me she would not be able to attract a quality guy. I rescued her from a low life!

The real kicker to this scenario is that Kathy had fit perfectly the "list" of positive qualities that I had been looking for in a wife. She was fun loving, pretty, smart, outgoing, wanted to minister with me, enjoyed singing and would be able to write books with me. God had given me everything that I had asked for in a wife and I was constantly belittling her and putting her down.

When Kathy makes a mistake now, I remind myself of a time I have made the same mistake. If I have not made that same mistake, I try to remind myself of something else I am working on in which Kathy is already strong.

Kathy is extremely busy with our four children, ministry, blessing me and being friends with everyone that she meets. If you need to be encouraged or counseled, just hint to Kathy that you have a need. She will pour her heart out in attempting to encourage you. I love this about Kathy.

The backside of both Kathy and me being busy in all of the activities is that we will sometimes forget details.

Here is a funny example of this. We were at the Hunter Healing Explosion in October of 2004 at the Houston Astrodome. Our good friends, Kenneth and Christine, were helping us man our book sales table. (You read Kenneth and Christine's wonderful testimony at the beginning of this book. They received an outstanding miracle of marriage restoration from reading *The Man of Her Dreams/The Woman of His!*)

When Kenneth and I arrived at the table, he remembered that he forgot his coffee at the hotel. He asked if I would call Kathy and see if she would bring the coffee when she came. Christine was skipping this meeting as she was tied up with their newborn.

Kenneth then asked me to add to Kathy's task, bringing some Claritin. I grinned and said, "Well Kenneth, this is not Kathy's strong point. I will ask her, but I make no promises. You might get coffee, you might get Claritin, you might get both, you might get neither!" I called Kathy, and as always, she was happy to oblige. The day progressed and we forgot all about the coffee and Claritin.

When we prepared to leave that night, Kathy exclaimed, "Kenneth! I have your coffee in the van!" As we began to laugh, I asked about the Claritin to which Kathy replied, "The Claritin? Oh! The Claritin! I forgot to get that!" I said to Kenneth through my laughter, "You got nothing!" If memory serves me right, I laughed so hard that I almost passed out!

The fact is that no one marries above or below his or her level. You may have **different weaknesses and different strengths** than your spouse, but you are neither superior nor inferior to them. Learn to roll with, appreciate and laugh at these differences.

The same Randy that we mentioned in the last chapter loves to say that he married below his level. He reminds me how scatterbrained Susan is. He reminds me that she loses things all of the time. He reminds me that she is a social butterfly who is very shallow while he is very serious and picks friends cautiously.

> **SOMEWHERE ALONG THE LINE, THE BODY OF CHRIST GOT THE IDEA THAT ONLY THE MALE OF OUR SPECIES IS MADE IN THE IMAGE OF GOD.**

I simply remind Randy that it was **he** who **committed adultery three times** and it is **his wife** who **has been faithful to him** for their 12+ years together. I tell him, "Randy, at your very **best** you are only Susan's equal. What you and I did to our wives makes us the lowest of all husbands!"

"Adultery is worse than physical abuse. The scars may not be outwardly evident but they go much deeper. Nothing can damage your wife emotionally more than knowing that the love of her life chose another woman. Susan dedicated her life to you and can no longer say that you have been hers alone since you have been married. Susan is an incredibly strong woman who is working on

forgiving you. She is giving you time to grow into an adult
male and hopefully a great husband someday."

Abusive men **always** think that they married
"down". This fantasy hides the fact that they are
desperately afraid of losing their spouses. The physical,
mental or emotional abuse is designed to keep their
spouse off balance so that they do not feel confident
enough to leave. This to the abusive man is his only hope
of keeping his wife.

As someone said, "If he would just be a great
husband, she wouldn't WANT to leave!" Yes, this is true.
By reading this book, an abusive husband can learn to be a
great husband. He does not have to lock his wife in by
degrading. He can lock her in by treating her with honor!

So God **created man** *in his image; in the image
of God He created him;* **male and female He
created THEM!**
Genesis 1:27

When God looks at your wife and you he sees your
union as his crowning creation: "Man". He sees you
together as one rather than two separate and individual
beings with different "roles" and "ranks". This "roles and
ranks" emphasis has been foundational in the Body of
Christ for years. It contributes nothing that positively
impacts a couple's marriage relationship. Instead, it
negatively contributes to justifying the controlling nature
with which Christian men seek to dominate their wives.
The emphasis needs to be re-examined and ultimately
discarded. It serves no productive purpose.

143

Physical abuse victim Tonya was seated with three pastors. They were discussing the relationship between men and women. One pastor made the comment; "God did create men and women equally but with different roles." Tonya's reply was quick and to the point. "Oh really? Were they cinnamon or Danish?"

Point taken. God made **man**. *Male* and *female* he created **them**. **Both are created equally.** Man is a general term for men **and** women. **Male and female together equals "man".**

Every man has his own unique justification for his controlling nature.

MALE AND FEMALE TOGETHER EQUALS "MAN".

Italian men say that they will be a "schlep" if they respect their wives and give them too much freedom.

Egyptian and **Moslem** men blame their controlling nature on their culture.

Men from many Latin cultures say that real men are independent. A little control and a half dozen affairs are just part of a normal relationship!

Christian men justify **their** controlling and manipulative nature by the usage of scripture.

Every man's controlling nature proceeds from the same fallen nature. Control and manipulation are the

144

result of the fall. "Your wife will have a desire for you and you will rule, like a dictatorial tyrant, over her."

Somewhere along the line, the Body of Christ got the idea that **only the male** of our species is made in the image of God and that as an **afterthought** He made a secondary, inferior person. Woman is **not really** made in the image of God. The impact of this belief is found in the ranks of Christian women who are suffering daily at the hands of their "God-fearing" husbands.

A sure sign that a man is being healed of his abusive tendencies is when he accepts the fact that his wife is not "below him". **She is his perfectly capable, comparable and God-ordained equal.** Your wife is not your "momma" and you are not her "old man". You are lovers, friends, teammates and equals.

God desires that you honor **Him** by **loving each other deeply.** You are not above your wife and she is not above you. You mutually adapt to one another and you grow into the man that God has called you to be by becoming the husband that she needs you to be.

GOLDEN KEY

YOU DID NOT
MARRY UP OR DOWN

Dear Joel and Kathy,

I received information on your book at the Global Pastors Network and Women in Ministry conference. After receiving the book, I immediately began to read. I could hardly put it down. It is so "on the money".

I recently completed two Doctoral degrees, one of which is in Education (university) with Specialization in Conflict Resolution and the other in Religious Education (seminary). In relation to this, I thoroughly researched domestic violence in the church. It is such a silenced issue, and many pastors are in denial. My dissertation will be looking at the African American communities... where the epidemic seems to be devastating.

I myself am a survivor. I am divorced and the "old" Joel is representative of my ex. It is scary to see the similarities and realize that these problems are widespread in the church! You are to be commended for taking responsibility for your actions, moving to a place of forgiveness and cleaning up the mess rather than wearing a "holy" mask. Pastors are put on pedestals, but Pastors are just men with a calling. They are not above making mistakes. It is, however, an admirable and respectful thing when you mess up, admit it, turn it around, and then use it to glorify God. God loves marriages! He said it is not good (desirable) for man to be alone... He wants us together! This book is absolutely mind-blowing!

I am lending a listening ear to a friend in crisis as we speak. Before coming to work today, her husband tried hard to aggravate her. He pushed all her buttons so she would react and become violent. This way he could feel like he's not the problem. I referred her to your book. God tells us in sacred Scripture "My people perish because of a lack of knowledge"(Hosea 4:6). There is no excuse to not gain this knowledge. You have definitely planted a seed; we each have a dynamic responsibility to water it (to read) and to carry the words of freedom to the lost.

Dr. Sandra Hamilton,
Miami, Florida

Chapter Thirteen

Shining
Your Crown

*An **excellent wife** is the **crown** of her husband.*

Proverbs 12:4

By Joel and Kathy

A crown to a king is his most prized and valuable possession. A king's crown is his glory. A king's crown represents him. A king's pride and joy is when his crown sparkles and shines. If his crown gets even a smudge, it is immediately cleaned to a sparkling shine again.

If my wife is my crown then I want her to shine! How can I shine her? I shine my crown by praising her. I shine my crown by building her up. I shine my crown by complimenting her.

As I build up Kathy she becomes very secure. When she is secure, the inner beauty that God has graced her with is poured out upon me! I reap the benefit! As I validate Kathy by reinforcing the high value that I place upon her she makes it her mission to be the best person that she can be! Kathy's confidence manifests itself in both inward and outward beauty! We have it easy, guys! God created our wives to desire us. When we treat them well they naturally blossom like a rose.

We want to shine our crowns. When we shine our wives, they in turn will search out ways to increase their shine value to us, both inwardly and outwardly.

For example, Kathy is a very good shopper. She can find very expensive and beautiful outfits at low prices by shopping in clean consignment and thrift shops. I have never resented her spending money to buy clothes! I want her to look and feel great! She is my crown!

Another expense that I never resent spending money on is make-up! Kathy **studies** make-up and fashion styles. As my crown I appreciate that she knows how to shine! One woman said to my wife, "I feel like God told me to tell you to throw away all of your fashion magazines. You are beautiful enough!" The visitor may have been complimenting my wife but I can guarantee that God was not telling Kathy to throw away all of her style and beauty magazines! (On the other hand, this second-time church visitor may have been trying to present her personal opinion as the voice of God! We never **did** see her again!)

> **I WANT HER TO LOOK AND FEEL GREAT! SHE IS MY CROWN!**

At a resort in Orlando that we once visited, the activities department offered a "Newlywed Game" poolside. We agreed to participate. We look for unusual daily opportunities to share principles of a happily married life with couples. One question was this: "What will your wife say that your answer would be to this question: 'What does your wife spend money on that she already has too much of?'" There were four options: shoes, knick-knacks, jewelry or make-up.

Each of the men wrote answers and we compared notes. We each had a great laugh about shoes being the obvious answer. All of the men present commented that they certainly don't mind it when their wives buy make-up and that they could not have too much!

Undoubtedly, our wives all knew the level of value that we each placed on make-up and the fact that we found it humorous that they each had at least 20 pairs of shoes!

Back came our wives! The first one answered confidently that her husband would have said that she spent too much on make-up! We husbands who remained looked at each other with a knowing look wondering how they could have possibly missed out on such easy points!

The second wife then confidently gave the same answer! Make-up! The rest of us were surprised and started laughing. Every single wife gave the same answer! Make-up! Every man rolled his eyes saying, "Sweetheart, I don't mind you spending money on make-up! You can't get too much of that! Shoes! The answer is shoes! You have twenty pairs!"

Finally, Kathy was the last of the wives to give her answer. We had already won the first round, punctuated by 60 second "mini-teachings" on marriage and we all knew that Kathy would get it right.

Kathy looked at me, looked at everyone else, paused a second and said, "Well, I know everyone else said make-up and got it wrong but I am going to say... 'Make-up!'" Everyone busted up laughing in hysterics. The moment was very funny! I was like, "Acck!" (We still went on to win round two! Our prize? We each received a plastic flower lei to wear around our necks! Woo-Hoo!) The best part was that we did get to speak some positive words into the lives of a handful of couples that we would never have met otherwise and probably will never see again!

Guys, if you expect your wife to dress sharply and look good, you have to be sure that she has money and that she has your blessing to spend that money on herself. This is especially important if you have children.

We have seen numerous instances where the husband and children were always dressed in nice new clothes while mom, placing herself on the bottom of the totem pole, is wearing clothes that are eight to ten years old. If your wife can't bring herself to spend money on herself, go on a shopping date together!

Remember, if funds are tight many upscale consignment shops offer upscale clothes for pennies on the dollar. These clothes are often beautiful and look like new. I cannot count the times that Kathy has modeled an incredible new shirt or outfit for me that she has bought at a nice re-sale shop. I will be thinking that it cost $100 on sale! When I ask what it cost she gives me the victorious announcement: "Two dollars!" The woman has a gift!

I appreciate it when Kathy looks really good and I appreciate it when she sometimes has a bit of a "sexy" edge to her outfit for the day. I much prefer looking at my own wife with interest rather than noticing other women! It would not be healthy for me to notice how nice another lady looks and then to look at Kathy, desiring that she dressed more appealing.

Revealing outfits are to the point of ridiculous in our world today. A Christian wife is not competing with the scantily clad, airbrushed, augmented billboard models that confront her husband every day. Having said that, most Christian husbands enjoy their wives looking "sexy," in a modest way, occasionally!

> **I MAKE A SPECIAL POINT TO LOOK AT KATHY AND WHISPER SWEET, FUN COMMENTS THAT COMPLIMENT HER ON HOW GOOD SHE LOOKS.**

Men in general notice attractive women. Period. End of story. Right or wrong. Good or bad. They just do. Charlie Shedd settled that issue many years ago in his classic work, "Letters to Phillip". Kathy does not mind that I notice. What she does mind though is that "second look!" Everyone knows what I mean by "second look!" You are **not** shining your crown when you make an effort for a second look. That second look devalues your wife instead of building her up.

I shine Kathy by enjoying *her* when she dresses in a way that keeps my attention! I make a special point to look at Kathy and whisper sweet, fun comments that compliment her on how good she looks! I enjoy lots of variety. I like it when Kathy dresses sharply for a special gathering. I like it when she is in jeans and an old sweatshirt on a cool day. I like it when she dresses upscale casually. I also like it when she is dressed comfortably in a way that won't cause her to drown in sweat on a hot, humid Southern day!

Kathy was told once by a "pastorette," as we like to call lady pastors, that she should wear dresses with hems below their knees. Kathy and I discussed this at length. Kathy had learned about dress length and body styles in her fashion studies.

Kathy is short and thin. She explained that her proper dress length was above the knees. If a short woman wears a dress below the knees her legs appear short and "stumpy". Being teachable I agreed with her that she should continue to wear dresses that complement her body type. The Bible says that a fool refuses instructions and what do I know about women's dress? Kathy should not have to wear dresses a certain length simply because it is the acceptable "religious" length. As the old saying goes, "We got saved and then we got religious." It is not acceptable in some religions for a woman to even reveal her arm! The men, however, are not held to the same standard.

I wondered about this occasionally until three years later. We were watching "What Not To Wear" on TLC. The guest was a woman with Kathy's exact build. I about fell out when I heard the hosts explain word for word what Kathy had said to me three years before. They told the guest to throw out her "below the knee" dresses! They said dresses below the knees on a short person make their legs look stumpy! Kathy notes that high heels will at times fix this problem but flats with dresses below the knees do not **ever** work for a short person, male or female!

A crown makes a king look good. The king is very proud of his crown and displays it to impress. You increase your wife's value when you brag on **her** as a king would brag about the **crown** that thrills **him** so.

> **YOU INCREASE YOUR WIFE'S VALUE WHEN YOU BRAG ON HER AS A KING WOULD BRAG ABOUT THE CROWN THAT THRILLS HIM SO.**

This is all about shining your wife! She is your crown! Be glad when she glows and looks beautiful.

Your wife's "glow" is representing to the world that her husband treats her with the same honor that he would treat a multi-million dollar crown! Build your wife up. She represents you! Encourage her to learn about fashion and style. Be happy when she is going out into the community looking good and representing you in style! Shine your crown always. She is the best part of you.

By Kathy

The Bible says that an excellent wife is the crown of her husband. I want to be an excellent wife and I want to be a crown that is just as valuable to my man as a crown is to a king! A crown represents the king's value! A crown makes a king look good! That is one of my goals as an excellent wife! To make my husband look good! I want him to be proud of me to the point that he brags and shows me off!

I think often of the story of Esther. The King had requested that Queen Vashti come to his party so that he could show her off! She refused and lost her throne! Why did the King summon her in the first place? Could it be that he was proud of his queen? Could it be that he felt blessed and honored to have such a wonderful wife? I am sure that she carried herself with an air of beautiful dignity and he wanted to brag a little about his good fortune!

In the same way that a woman dreams about her man **treating her** like a queen, a man dreams about **having a beautiful queen** on his arm when they are walking together!

Just like **you** want to **brag** to your lady friends about how **wonderfully** your husband is treating you, **he** wants to think to himself, **"Eat your heart out. She's all mine!"**

To choose his next Queen, the King held a beauty pageant. Esther was given "beauty preparations" and an allowance for the competition. Esther was already beautiful! Her beauty is what had landed her the opportunity to enter the competition! She did not rest on her laurels, though. Seven choice maidservants were assigned to work on Esther for a **year!** There was some **serious** "beautification" going on!

Esther spent six months soaking in Oil of Myrrh and another six months with other perfumes and beauty preparations. We cannot spend a year soaking in perfumes and oil of myrrh but we **can regularly improve our appearance.** Just the fact that you are working on it regularly qualifies you as "The Woman of His". Your man will be thrilled that you are getting better looking every day! You have not given up!

> **WHO GETS THE CREDIT WHEN THE CROWN IS SHINING? YOUR HUSBAND! YOU WILL SHINE IN DIRECT RELATION TO HOW YOU ARE BEING TREATED BEHIND CLOSED DOORS.**

Every marriage book emphasizes a woman's inner beauty. Suffice to say that it is not good for a woman to be ugly, mean, unkind and unmerciful on the inside. It has been proven time and again that these negative attributes in a wife's personality will "go away" when a man becomes the husband that his wife needs him to be. A wife who is a believer and wants to please God **will be beautiful on the inside** as her husband becomes the man that God has called him to be! **It is hard to be beautiful on the inside if your husband is tarnishing your self-image daily!**

A shining crown will be beautiful on the inside and will utilize everything that she has been given by God to be beautiful for her husband on the outside. Who gets the credit when the crown is shining? Your husband! You will shine in direct relation to how you are being treated behind closed doors.

Enhance Your Husband!

A crown enhances the king who wears it. My goal is to enhance my husband. I want to do simple things like making him a cup of coffee or bringing him a glass of juice. I do things that lift his load when I am able. Asking him if there is anything that I can do to help him is another way to enhance his day.

I always make it a point to look my best. I put makeup on everyday and dress in ways that are pleasing to him. If you have certain clothes that your husband does not like, my question is "Why would you wear it?" If my husband does not like an outfit, out it goes! Sometimes I will work with it to make it look nice but if it still does not "turn him on", out it goes!

I also make it a point to look good when we go to bed. Years ago I read that Lynette Hagin's husband, Ken Jr. had not seen her without make-up! She went to bed in make-up, got up to remove it after he fell asleep and rose before Ken in the morning to reapply. I do not do that but I always look good for Joel! You don't have to go overboard, but if your husband says that he does not care how you look when you go to bed, don't believe him! I don't go to bed in hair rollers or flannel PJ's! You will never find me displaying an attitude of "I don't care how I look". There are times that the day gets going before the make-up goes on but at the first opportunity I will be at the mirror "beautifying!"

Speaking of bedtime, Joel and I go to bed at the same time 90% of the time. How can you stay close to your husband if you do not have this important time of fellowship?

If Joel is in the bedroom and I have to change clothes, do you think that I change in the bathroom? No way! This is just another chance to have fun in daily life! He will normally look up from what he is doing and say something to the effect of "Now that is just plain not fair! You are doing that on purpose! You are just too gorgeous. You would think that I could focus on (reading, working, studying) but no... You come and change clothes right in my line of view!" I just love it!

> **PART OF THE REASON HE MARRIED YOU WAS TO GET TO SEE YOU IN VARIOUS STATES OF DRESS OR UNDRESS!**

Some wives we have met were shy about disrobing in front of their husband. That is just not right! Part of the reason he married you was to get to see you in various states of dress or undress! Don't take that away from your husband. **That** is just not fair. When these shy ladies have thrown caution to the wind they have reported much happier husbands!

On a final note, I suggest that you occasionally visit clothing stores such as Victoria's Secret. (Without your husband!) These stores also offer mail order catalogs. Just keep them hidden from your husband's sight! Trust me. He will thank you. Remember? *The **Man** of **Her** Dreams/*

The **Woman** *of* **His!** We are trusting that your husband will become the man of **your** dreams. These are some little things that you can do to be the **woman** of his!

Another way that I add to my man's life is that I am upbeat. I stay happy and create lots of fun. Some men seem to be annoyed if their wives are upbeat. What is this all about? Would they prefer it if she were depressed? I would hope not! I sing. I laugh a lot. I play jokes on Joel and the kids. We keep love games going which keep us fresh, fun and alive.

Think about your husband. What does he like? What can you do that would enhance his day? Have you been complimenting your husband lately? Do you tell him in many ways that he is the **only man in your world**? Does he know that you appreciate his hard work when he accomplishes a goal? Are you his cheerleader? Does your man really feel like you respect him as a "hunk of man?"

These are all very simple ways that you can build your husband up and enhance him. These are ways that you can be that excellent wife who is a crown to her husband!

GOLDEN KEY

WHEN THE CROWN IS SHINING
EVERYONE BENEFITS!

Chapter Fourteen

Submit?
Adapt?

Submitting to one another in the fear of
God.

Ephesians 5:21

By Joel

Submit. Adapt. Submit. Adapt. Submit? Adapt?
What is this all about? Frankly, Kathy and I like to use the
word "adapt" in place of the word "submit". Why? One
reason is that "adapt" is a friendly word which more
accurately reflects the biblical intention of the word.

The word "submit" for many people has a negative
connotation.

In the early 60's, teaching about marriage became
popular in the Body of Christ. The emphasis was placed
solely upon the woman to "submit" to her husband; the
man of the house; the head of the home; the king of the
castle. Women were expected to be everything and do
everything that her husband could ever hope or want
regardless of how he acted and treated her.

The wife was never to complain or argue and was
instructed to constantly tell him how wonderful he was. If
the dutiful, submissive wife were ever to try to "usurp his
authority" by asking him why he was home late for dinner

or what he spent all the money on then she was "in rebellion."

When I was a lad, our family went to what I recall as a wonderful Christian camp for two summer vacations. It was fun for me. I went fishing every morning at 6 a.m. There were Sunday school classes during the day, cute girls to chase around, new friends to meet and church in the evenings. I requested to be baptized in Leech Lake when they had the camp baptism service. At the end of the week, there was a big fish fry where we ate all of the fish that the men had caught. (Note: The **Ladies** cleaned the fish!)

My mom's experience was a little different than mine. When we talk about those days now, she refers to it as the "submission camp". My 9-year-old mind did not realize that the ministry was all about teaching women to submit to their husbands!

My mother **clearly** remembers the day that she had her six kids at the rustic campground and found herself wondering where her pastor-husband was. She had two children in diapers and a U-haul full of stuff to get settled into the cabin. She could not find my dad anywhere.

She asked the camp director's wife if she knew where he was and she said, "Oh, they went to Minneapolis to pick up supplies. They will be back in a couple days!" My mom, being quite surprised, said, "He did? He did not tell me he was leaving." The "submissive" woman replied, "Oh. The men don't have to tell us where they are going. They can just leave." So, there my mom was for two days in a strange camp with her six children. This was her introduction to "submission".

On the way back from Minneapolis, the trailer that the men were using to bring supplies disengaged and the supplies were strewn all over the road! Served the heels right! I don't think God was happy with all of this submission stuff!

The Camp Zion "ministry" taught that the wife was to kneel at her husband's feet and the husband was to put his hands on his wife's head and speak over her every night! They were instructed that whatever their husband said was the voice of God to them! My mother clearly remembers kneeling at my dad's feet in obedience to what was taught!

What a dream for a husband! No responsibility to his wife! She has to obey every word he says as **if God himself were speaking!** He can **come** and **go** and **do** as he pleases and if his wife **ever** says a word she is **in rebellion** to the Word of God! **Woo Hoo!** The recently renovated/regurgitated teaching that a husband is "God's delegated authority" over his wife is not a fresh revelation for 2008! It is old error from the sixties and early 1970's!

At the end of one of these weeks, my dad stood up and joyfully gave his public praise report! He had suffered with pain in his neck and now that his wife had learned submission the pain was gone! He now realized that the pain had not been anything physical. (In other words, my mom had been a pain in the neck!)

At least I and my five brothers and sisters enjoyed the week! Well, I guess my dad did, too! That about sums up the wrong emphasis on submission. Everyone has fun at the wife and mother's expense. She carries the load of everything, all the while being treated poorly by her husband!

Many women will remember the book *Total Woman* by Marabel Morgan. This young lady of about 30 years of age stormed the country with her best selling book and appeared on many national TV programs with her **revolutionary message** of submission. Her theory? If only the wife were to do **everything perfect**, then her husband would become a responsible, loving husband and they would have a wonderful marriage.

> **IF ONLY THE WIFE WERE TO DO EVERYTHING PERFECT, THEN HER HUSBAND WOULD BECOME A RESPONSIBLE, LOVING HUSBAND AND THEY WOULD HAVE A WONDERFUL MARRIAGE.**

I don't think so. There **were** testimonies of husbands who indeed were pleasantly surprised at the change in their wives. She recommended lots of fun sex, cute outfits, adoring words and beautifully prepared meals with no negative words, thoughts or feelings ever to be projected toward the husband. I still like the fun sex, cute outfits, adoring words and Kathy's cooking! Let's not throw the baby out with the bath water!

We teach that women are **designed by God** to **desire** their husbands. **If** a **husband** will **lay his life down** for his wife and meet **her** needs, she will **want** to do these things for him. She won't be **forcing** herself in order to keep peace and appease him. Yes, there may be an uncomfortable season of healing needed before a wife can "go there" – to that place of "wanting" to respond warmly and positively to a husband, but regardless of the necessary time, that is the end result. Our second book, *Livin' It and Lovin' It!* covers this process in detail.

Our emphasis requires that the husband grow up! It requires that the husband care for and love his wife. It requires that he listen to her heart and meet her needs as she expresses them. We think that this emphasis makes for much better long-term marriages which produce **two** happy campers instead of **one** happy camper who is a selfish "twit" and one **self-sacrificing** wife who never asks the husband to do anything except enjoy being "the king."

I personally **loved** *Total Woman*! It told my wife that she was obviously not doing enough to make our marriage a happy marriage. **If only she did enough** then **I** would not be verbally, emotionally or spiritually abusive! This **would** work for a while until Kathy would get fed up with being pushed around and finally explode. Then she would beat herself up because she failed in her goal of being submissive! I, of course, consistently reinforced this perception! All of the women we have met who tried *The Total Woman* philosophy report that their marriages **initially improved but ultimately went downhill.** Gail read and lived *The Total Woman,* yet only saw her husband get worse. She says, "I have come to the conclusion that men are about the emotional age of **ten** and that if you cater to them, enabling them to never grow up, they only get better for a short time. Eventually, they will lose all respect for you and become **more** of a tyrant, **more** demanding, **more** selfish and **more** childish than they ever were before you began reading *The Total Woman*."

The biblical usage of the word **"submit"** is most often translated from the Greek word **"hupotasso"**. We find "Hupotasso" in Ephesians 5:21. ***"Submitting yourselves one to another".*** The word means "to subordinate, to obey, to be subject to and to submit oneself to." In the very next verse we find these words:

> **Wives, submit to your own husbands,** *as to the Lord.*
>
> *Ephesians 5:22*

The net effect of this double usage of the word "submit" in back to back verses is that men totally ignore the fact that verse 21 requires **mutual submission.** The word "submit" therefore has only been applied to the wife submitting to her husband. Haven't you heard? "A husband is **never** told to submit to his wife. Heresy!"

The word "submit," as found in the preceding verses, has for years been mistakenly taught as being the exclusive responsibility of the wife in a Christian marriage.

A foundation of teaching was built – and has been sustained since the early 60's - that a woman was solely responsible for the success or failure of her marriage. This theory is that if a woman will only submit enough to her husband, her submission will tame the beast and he will not be abusive toward her. For years this was the complete emphasis of all marriage teaching in the church. A woman was to relegate herself to being a doormat to be walked upon with a smile on her face, a song in her voice and dinner on the stove while at all times being ready for rollicking good times in the bedroom!

The sad result was that this misguided emphasis simply gave men a **new way to abuse their wives.** Now they had the **Bible** behind them. A husband could yell and scream at his wife and say it was because she was not submissive. He could be immature, not clean up after himself, stay out all night, and spend the family's money. If his wife were to object he could tell her she was in rebellion. If he wanted to pull out the big guns he would claim that she had a "Jezebel" spirit.

Of course, most pastors agreed with the husbands. Most pastors were men. Their wives **were** rebellious. In some churches it could be reported that **every single woman** was a carrier of the "Jezebel spirit". This new form of abuse has been coined "spiritual abuse." It goes on today behind the closed doors of Christian homes (and churches) more than anyone would ever want to admit.

Instead of **physically** beating a wife into submission, the "spiritual" man could use the **Bible** to beat his wife into submission to his immature demands. He could control every little detail of their life together and of whatever life she might try to squeeze out for herself.

165

We know of one pastor who so needed to control his wife's every move that he installed a **pay phone** in the parsonage! In those days calls were ten cents so the "loving husband and pastor" would ration the dimes as he chose. Another pastor we know would so beat his wife physically that he would have to read his sermons word for word. He would be in the pulpit shaking to the point that he could not hold a Bible or microphone. He would simply lay his word-for-word sermons out on the pulpit and read while he held tightly onto its sides.

> **INSTEAD OF PHYSICALLY BEATING HIS WIFE INTO SUBMISSION, THE SPIRITUAL MAN COULD USE THE BIBLE TO BEAT HIS WIFE INTO SUBMISSION.**

Both of these pastors believed that the reason they acted this way was because their wives were not in "submission" to them.

Rachel told us her story: "I was counseled by my pastor to stay in a physically and emotionally abusive marriage. He used me to go to the homes of other abused women and encourage them to continue to receive the beatings, remain humble and pray. This kept the numbers and 'appearances' up in church." Rachel continued, "I phoned the pastor in the middle of a beating. When it was over my husband left. The pastor was still on the line and was angry with me that I called him to listen. He told me of a woman who was beaten for 20 years until her husband was saved and he said that if I would submit, my husband would also get saved someday."

"That was enough for me. I fasted 3 days, and then my husband left. He later came back in tears begging to be restored. I refused. Soon it was revealed that he had been in adultery with a 15-year-old girl in the church. He has lived with several women since and is still not serving the Lord. At least he is not putting on a show to pretend he is a Christian anymore." Abuse of any kind is a tragedy. Be sure that you are not acting abusively toward the wife of your youth. You might lose her.

If your wife is solely responsible for the success of your marriage, what is there left for you to do? When I realized that I was waiting for Kathy to be the perfect wife, I was shocked. Here I was; the "Man of God with the Power for the Hour" and the only answer I had for our problems was to blame Kathy, claiming that she was just not submissive enough. I abused her spiritually on a regular basis, using Bible verses to "hit" her with, or at the very least, to hold her in "check". When I learned to listen to her heart, mutually adapt (submit) to her, and meet her needs, our marriage was miraculously restored to the outrageously happy relationship we enjoy today.

GOLDEN KEY

THE MAN OF HER DREAMS
LISTENS TO HER HEART
AND FULFILLS HER DESIRES

Dear Joel and Kathy,

In November, we held a Glamour Shots Women's Retreat in which one of our church members took pictures for us to give to our loved ones for Christmas. Our pastor's wife was there and received a phone call that her son had shot himself with a gun. Tragically, he passed away. You might remember my sharing this story on the stage at the National Christian Counselors Association Conference in Orlando.

We had another retreat in January to make up for the one that was tragically cut short in November. Seventeen women attended the retreat. We again took Glamour Shots, this time for Valentine's Day. Now the plot thickens...

After we had eaten dinner, we were all sitting around in a circle. I began to tell the story of our meeting in Orlando, your fabulous book, and the story about my mom and dad, brother, and husband. They loved it! But of course they would; after all, we were taking romantic pictures for Valentine's Day! What better time to tell the story, right? Well, when I got to the end, I popped out 17 copies of your book and said, "And everybody gets a book!" They broke into laughter. Some cried! Some even shouted, "It's an Oprah moment!" It was soooo wonderful! I can't wait to hear their testimonies. Thought you'd like to know that I'm about my Father's business!

In His Wonderful Romantic Love that only He can give,
Angela

<u>*Authors' Note*</u>
If you, too, would like to be about your Father's business by helping troubled marriages, there are multiple copy discount prices listed in the front of the book and at our web site: www.joelandkathy.com. You can be a carrier of marriage miracles and restoration!

Chapter Fifteen

Adapting To One Another

Submitting to one another in the fear of God.

Ephesians 5:21

Wives, **submit to your own husbands,** *as to the Lord.*

Ephesians 5:22

By Joel

The word "submit" which is translated from the Greek word "hupotasso" is found in Ephesians 5:21. It is used in reference to submitting **one to another**. The very next verse then goes on to repeat the English word "submit," instructing wives **specifically** to submit to their husbands.

I always found this to be very odd. Why would God tell believers to submit one to another and then immediately tell wives separately and specifically to submit to their husbands? The way my Bible reads is like this: **"Submitting yourselves to one another. Wives, submit to your own husbands as to the Lord."** This just does not make any sense. In general, if the Bible does not make sense, there is something lost in the translation. That surely is the case here.

Wives, **submit** *to your own husbands, as to the Lord.*

Ephesians 5:22

"Submit" in this verse is **not** the word **"hupotasso"** being repeated, as it seems. Here comes the definition of this word for submit. The Greek word is a little different from the word "hupotasso". Are you ready for this? Be sure to **read slowly** and emphasize each and every word! The definition, according to Thayer's Greek Dictionary is:

"Inserted word: This word was added by the translators for better readability in the English. There is no actual word in the Greek text!"

(Thayer's #9999)

You have got to be kidding me! No, I am not kidding. And it gets even better. If you take the word "submit" out of the verse, it reads like this: **"Wives, unto your own husbands as unto the Lord"**. The word translated "unto your own" is the word "idios" which means, "pertaining to self, one's own, private or separate."

(Strong's #2398)

The verse would be literally translated much better if you read it like this:

Let the wife be private and separate to her husband as she is to the Lord.

Now this makes sense. Anyone can understand this. "Submit one to another and you wives, be private and separate unto your own husband as unto the Lord. Be

170

faithful to your husband. Be set apart solely for him. Don't let another man get into your 'space'. Your space is reserved exclusively for your husband." One thing that has always impressed me about Kathy is how private and separate that she is to me. I often thought that Kathy would be tempted to have an affair after I did. This is not how Kathy thinks or acts. She has had opportunities at vulnerable times yet has maintained herself private and separate. It is awe-inspiring to see and I am grateful for this quality in her.

> **BE SET APART SOLELY FOR HIM. DON'T LET ANOTHER MAN GET INTO YOUR SPACE. YOUR SPACE IS RESERVED EXCLUSIVELY FOR YOUR HUSBAND.**

Certainly Kathy had times when she could have gone that direction. The years that I resisted meeting her needs were a perfect set up. The first few months after the adultery were also a vulnerable time. Kudos to every woman who, like Kathy, stays faithful to God and to her man even in the face of legitimate, unmet emotional needs.

A normal Christian woman will never commit adultery if her husband **is** meeting her emotional needs. Men are not like this. Guys will commit adultery even if their wife is a "10" in looks and attitude toward him. Adultery for men is clearly a character issue. If a man is going to commit adultery, he is going to commit adultery. It simply does not matter how wonderful his wife is nor does it have anything to do with how well or how poorly his wife treats him.

If the husband met her emotional needs she would be treating him well anyway. This has nothing to do with his character flaw. The fact remains: A wife's poor treatment of him is simply a convenient excuse for the man who commits adultery. He would have committed adultery even if his wife had treated him like a king. Sorry guys. Truth hurts. I had to swallow it in order to grow up and so do you.

> **A FEW COMPLIMENTS, SOME FLOWERS AND A LISTENING EAR ARE A HEAVY TEMPTATION FOR THE WOMAN WHO IS MARRIED TO A HEEL!**

Women are **designed** to be "private and separate" unto their husbands as unto the Lord. The desire for her husband that God has placed in every wife will keep her faithful. If the husband refuses to meet her needs over an extended period of time, he is exposing his wife to the temptation to have her emotional needs met by the next man who is looking for some recreation. A few compliments, some flowers and a listening ear are a heavy temptation for the woman who is married to a heel! Unlike men, women generally will not commit adultery if their needs are being met. Women simply do not have "recreational" affairs.

Wives, stay private and separate unto your husband as unto the Lord.

This I can understand. This makes sense.

We are aware that there are isolated instances where a woman (as well as a man) may be bound by drugs, satanic influence or deep emotional scars that may propel them toward an affair. Let us address these unusual, but highly difficult circumstances directly.

Though we cannot change the past, and recovery may take time, we believe that even these serious issues can be healed in most cases if a husband will dedicate himself to meeting his wife's needs. When this very special couple has found a place of complete healing and restoration, God will be able to use them to bring the miracle of restoration to others just as He has to them.

God puts couples together through His divine providence. We believe that God handpicked you for your wife, and your wife for you. Why? One of the reasons for your union is the entire premise of this book. God knew exactly what your wife's needs would be and He knew that you would feel completely inadequate to meet them. God created your wife to express her feelings, so, outside of your wife being uniquely non-verbal or conditioned to your not meeting her expressed needs, she will express her feelings. This would be the signal for the old man in you to recoil, rebel, run and hide or fight back.

You now have the opportunity to crucify that old man by dying to yourself and meeting your wife's needs. When you learn to meet your wife's particular needs and you are enjoying a happy, fulfilled marriage, you will have grown into the man that God has called you to be. The solution is the same. Dying to yourself and meeting your wife's needs so that she is free to love you in return.

Mutual Submission

There **are** later **legitimate** uses of the word "hupotasso" as relating to wives but it is always in **tandem** with a **mutual submission, respect, adaptation** and **love**. For example:

SUBMIT IS A LOVING WORD THAT WOULD BE INTERPRETED BETTER AS "TO ADAPT" OR TO SIMPLY FLOW TOGETHER AS A TEAM, PREFERRING ONE ANOTHER.

*Wives, submit to your own husbands, as is fitting in the Lord. **Husbands, love your wives** and do not be bitter toward them.*
Colossians 3:18-19

Here the word "submit" is used in tandem with husbands being instructed to love their wives. We look at husbands loving their wives in Chapter 17.

Then "hupotasso" is used as it relates to a team ministry such as in a church service.

*For you can all prophesy one by one that all may learn and all may be encouraged. And the **spirits of the prophets are subject** to the prophets.*
1 Corinthians 14:31-32

This is simply telling us that a prophet does not **have** to speak when he has a word. He instead can choose to flow in harmony and wait his turn to speak.

Next, the Bible uses the word "hupotasso" in regards to submitting to leadership as in this example:

> *...They have devoted themselves to the ministry of the saints—that you also* **submit to such,** *and to everyone who works and labors with us.*
> *1 Corinthians 16:15-16*

This again is a request to work together as a team, flowing in love, joy, peace and unity. Remember our opening verse at the beginning of this chapter?

> **Submitting to one another.**
> *Ephesians 5:21*

In 1 Peter the word "hupotasso" is used again, reminding everyone to be submissive to one another.

> **Yes, all of you be submissive to one another** *and be clothed with* **humility.**
> *1 Peter 5:5b*

Same word: "hupotasso". That about says it all. Everyone should walk in a spirit of harmony, a spirit of adapting. We should all get along without anyone demanding his or her own way. We should look out for the interest of others and not just for "number one." That is what the word "hupotasso" is communicating.

The following verse seems to contradict this. It is commonly referred to by husbands and teachers when asserting that **husbands alone** are supposed to **rule** their homes and that their wives are supposed to **obey** them.

> *That they admonish the young women to love their husbands, to love their children, to be discreet, chaste, keepers at home, good,* **obedient to their husbands.**
>
> *Titus 2:4-5*

"WAIT! STOP RIGHT THERE! WIVES ARE SUPPOSED TO BE OBEDIENT TO THEIR HUSBANDS! I KNEW THAT VERSE WAS IN THERE SOMEWHERE! HA! CAN'T ARGUE WITH THAT! I AM DA BOSSMAN!" Oh yes. There it **is.** Spiritually abusive husbands **love** to emphasize **this!**

What you must realize is that the word for "obey" in this passage is simply "hupotasso." Nothing more. Nothing less. Yes, it is still the very same word that directs husbands and wives to submit to one another and instructs believers to submit to their church leaders. So there you have it, Mr. Control. Can **you** submit to this?

The Bible tells **you** to **submit** to your wife, your pastor and church elders. How far do **you** want to go in **"obeying"** your wife and pastor? If you want to utilize this verse to **demand obedience** from your wife then you must be willing to **render unto her** the **same level of obedience** you require of her and submit to demands for that same level of obedience from your pastor and church elders.

Kind of puts a different face on the word doesn't it? You want to be gently led by your Pastor, don't you? You want to have the freedom to disagree with him, don't you? You want free will to tell him no if he asks you to do something that you do not want to do, don't you? You want your wife to sweet talk to you when she asks you to do things for her, don't you? "Give me some sugar honey." Right?

You have to **"obey"** your wife and your pastor with the **same Greek word that tells your wife to "obey" you!** If your pastor asked you to do something that you did not want to do and went so far as to "demand your obedience" in the way that you like to demand your wife's obedience, you would probably just quit the church and find a new one! Okay. Have it your way.

> **YOU HAVE TO OBEY YOUR WIFE AND YOUR PASTOR WITH THE SAME GREEK WORD THAT TELLS YOUR WIFE TO OBEY YOU!**

If **you** want to **command your wife** like the **big boss** and demand **her** obedience, perhaps she should simply quit **you** and find another **husband!** I am being facetious here obviously.

The verses telling wives to submit to their husbands are **not** to be used against wives in order to force them to put up with abusive behavior from their husband. Submit is a loving word that would be interpreted better as "to adapt" or to simply "flow together as a team, preferring one another".

A very simple example is the one that Kathy shares about learning to enjoy football. When we were first married, Kathy did not like football. It had never been a part of her "world". She started watching it with me and ended up liking it. She adapted to me. Watching a football game together now is one of our special times together. We both love it!

There are many ways that a husband and wife can adapt to one another. He can learn to enjoy shopping trips! She can learn to fish! He can come to appreciate her friends. She can say "Yes, let's do that!" when he comes up with a "crazy" idea. He can return the favor when the "crazy" idea is hers.

She can try to enjoy car shows.

He can learn how to cook.

Adapting to one another, that is the goal.
The two becoming one.

GOLDEN KEY

BEGIN TODAY TO ADAPT TO ONE ANOTHER

Something to Think About

WE DID NOT SAY...

Repeat after us, men! "Joel and Kathy did *not say* that my wife is not required by scripture to submit to me. They have only affirmed that the Word instructs that a wife *is* to submit to her husband. However, Joel and Kathy have *ADDED* to this the rest of the truth: I am to mutually submit to my wife in the exact same manner that I expect her to submit to me. My wife is not required to submit to me *more* than I submit to her, and I am not required to submit to her *more* than she submits to me! *There is no 'big me' and there is no 'little you!'"*

Repeat after us, men! "Joel and Kathy did not say that I am not supposed to be the head of our home. They clearly affirmed that the Bible does indeed teach that a husband *is* supposed to be the head of his home. Joel and Kathy ADDED to this that my wife is *also* authorized by scripture to be the head of our home. I am not the 'higher authority' leader and my wife is not the 'higher authority' leader. We are authorized by God to lead our home as one flesh, as a unified team, with one mind, and with two hearts beating as one."

Paul declared that men are to love their wives as Christ loved the church. They are to lay *their* lives down for *their wives* as *Christ* laid *His* life down for the church. The disciples were no doubt stunned, in shock and in awe. They *witnessed* the passion of Christ first hand – up close and personal. They watched Jesus get beat to a bloody pulp. They stood by in horror as He carried and then hung on that same cross, naked, unrecognizable and rejected by God. They were eyewitnesses to this love that their beloved Jesus expressed to His bride, the church. They *watched Jesus* lay *His* life down for *His* bride.

I am sure that they reeled with this information, asking in disbelief, "How can *we*, as mere men, *possibly* lay our lives down for *our* wives as completely as Christ laid His life down for the church? This will take a lifetime of dedication to my wife. At best, I will not come close to what I saw Jesus just do because He so loved *His* bride."

Jesus did not look up from the ground and say, "If you do not submit to me, I will not die for you." No. Jesus did not do that. He just *died* for His bride, *regardless* of her response. Yes, Jesus had the *hope* laid before Him that she would respond by loving and serving Him in return, but *there were no guarantees*. He had to die. *First. With no strings attached.* This is how a husband is to love his wife. There are no guarantees, but there **is** a promise, and this promise is that your wife will have a desire for you. (Genesis 3:16) This is a promise you can count on. But, you must die **first.** You must lay your life down for your wife **first.**

Do you see why traditional marriage teachings have failed the church? The church has taught for *more* than an entire generation that the success or failure of a marriage was solely dependent on a wife's willingness to lay **her** life down in complete submission and service to her husband. (A generation is 40 years.) Women have been taught that if they will submit completely to their husband and follow his leadership in everything, that God would deal with him and that someday, he would be a good husband. It did not matter if he treated her rudely, yelled at her, called her names, or even treated her worse than his dog. She was simply to submit and pray.

This failed paradigm required a wife to function in the role of the *husband,* laying *her* life down for *him* as Christ laid His life down for the church. **The church, for over 45 years, has taught marriage completely backwards!** Is there any wonder that we have a 50% plus divorce rate in the church!

I guarantee that never once did an early church husband say to his wife, "You have to submit to me!" What an insult this would have been to the pain, agony and suffering that this husband witnessed Jesus go through for the church. When I hear a man declare, *"My wife has to submit to me!"* I want to scream at him in righteous anger, "How *dare* you worry about whether or not your wife is submitting to you? Have you *died* for her yet? Have you *suffered* in meeting *her* needs to the extent that *Jesus* suffered in dying for *you?* How *dare* you *insult* the blood of Jesus by demanding submission, when you have not yet begun to lay your life down for your wife in loving her, validating her, listening to her feelings, meeting her needs and serving her?"

John 3:16 says, "For God so loved the world that He gave His only begotten Son." When you have given yourself to your wife, in accordance with John 3:16, then you can stand on the promise of Genesis 3:16. Your wife *will* have a desire for you. She will love you, cherish you and respect you, in response to your "agape" love. It may take time if you have been a major heel for a number of years, but it will work. You have a Bible promise to stand on.

Chapter Sixteen

Desiring
Your Husband
Is A Good Thing

*Your **desire** shall be **for your husband.***
Genesis 3:16

By Kathy

We want women to have a **desire** for their husbands. Our aim is to help a man become the **husband** his wife **needs** him to be so that he can become the **man** that **God** has **called him** to become. If he will **do** this, his wife will fall back in love with him! What godly wife does not **hungrily desire a man who is everything that God has called him to be?**

Every woman wants a man who treats her like a queen. Every woman wants a man who places her in the rightful position of number one in his life (with only God being more supreme). We teach men that they **cannot claim** to love God if they do not **intensely love** their wife. We boldly teach women that if her husband truly loves God then he will truly love her as a result.

A man **demonstrates** his love for God by how well he loves his wife and children. Every woman wants a man who listens to her, is gentle and kind to her and supports her financially, spiritually, mentally and emotionally. Every woman wants a man who only has eyes for her.

If you are this woman then you will feel free to **desire** your husband. God **wants** you to desire your husband, communicate with him, serve him, bless him and spend time with him. This is God's desired response from you toward your godly and loving husband.

Think back to when you were first married. You **desired** your husband didn't you? Of course you did! You desired your husband and you were proud of that fact. You **bragged** to your friends about this wonderful guy you met. You laid awake at night thinking how **wonderful** it would be to marry this "knight in shining armor." **All of your childhood dreams were coming true!** You thought about him constantly. You **dreamed** about that perfect, secure, safe, romantic "happily ever after" life with this **perfectly wonderful, delightful** man.

> **A MAN DEMONSTRATES HIS LOVE FOR GOD BY HOW WELL HE LOVES HIS WIFE AND CHILDREN.**

You did not get married to "test him out" for a year or two and "see if it would work out." (If you did, you had some serious problems in your outlook on life!) You were marrying the man of your dreams! You were embarking on a new and exciting journey of romance and love, children, homes, security, joy and peace.

At some point after your wedding day you made the discovery that you were married to Dr. Jekyll and Mr. Hyde. To your dismay, you found out that sometimes **you** were **Mrs.** Jekyll and **Mrs.** Hyde! You had no idea that a man could bring such bad behavior out of you!

You found yourself arguing with your now "**bad dream**-boat" in the preferred method that you as a couple chose: cold shoulders, screaming, hitting, shaming, blaming and shifting blame, withholding sex, disappearing, manipulating, controlling. However the two of you chose to fight, it was not pretty. It never is. Your man violated you and you violated him in return. Your man did not listen to your heart and therefore had to listen to you rage. Perhaps you were abused physically, mentally, emotionally, or spiritually.

Hurt over and over again, you felt cheated by life. The dream you had as a young girl became a distant memory. Now when you see a kind and loving gentleman you fantasize over what "could have been" had you met him instead of the heel you know as your husband!

You are now living in a **cold war** with this man that you don't feel much for. Oh yes, you do have some good times. You go out with friends and/or to church. You laugh, you play, you eat together and you take the kids to ballgames. You are living life but there is **no passion!** There is no **love play!** There is no **excitement** about meeting each other in bed tonight. You are two people who live together, accomplish life together, raise children together and go to church but you are **not** two passionate lovers.

You would **not** describe yourself as being madly, wildly or radiantly in love. Those are the **last words** that you would use to describe your marriage. "Who? Tom and me? Wildly and radiantly in love with each other? I don't think so! We **put up** with each other, **sometimes!** We **survive** each other. We **might** make it until death do us part and we might **not. Who knows?** I really don't believe in divorce but we really are incompatible. At least we are staying together until the kids are grown. That is staying together longer than most couples."

Now your husband is reading this book. **Suddenly** he is telling you that he cares about your feelings. **Suddenly** he is helping you with the children and with the dishes. **Suddenly** he is working and paying the bills. Suddenly he is asking **you** to tell **him** what **he** needs to do differently in order **to become the husband that you need him to be!** Suddenly he is **doing those things** that you **begged him to do** years ago in futility until you finally **gave up trying!**

> **MAYBE IT GETS YOU REALLY ANGRY THAT HE SUDDENLY WANTS TO DO THE RIGHT THING.**

Maybe you don't **want** to tell him what he can do to become the husband you used to dream about! Maybe that hurts too much. Maybe it gets you really angry that he **suddenly** wants to do the right thing. After **ignoring, belittling and humiliating you** for years, he suddenly wants to become your **knight in shining armor?** Maybe you don't **want** him to be your knight in shining armor!

How are you going to handle this? It might take some soul searching. You might find yourself struggling with some very justifiably angry and bitter thoughts. Every time he does something nice you might get visions of him yelling at you, hitting you, ignoring you or being with the other woman.

This is not easy. We will not try to tell you that it will be easy. At some point, assuming he continues to prove his sincerity, you will **have** to let the defensive walls slowly come down and risk letting him into your heart again.

You might find yourself testing him out a bit. That would be understandable. A control-freak will not agree. He will say that you should just trust him at face value. You know better. You know what he is capable of.

Joel used to demand instant forgiveness and restoration from me. When Joel apologized, it was "end of story". I could not share my feelings about how his mistreatment made me feel. I could not ask him for complete closure. It was Joel's way or the highway!

Even after the adultery. Joel insisted that because he had repented, I was never to bring the issue up again. I had to suffer the emotional pain caused by adultery and was not allowed to ask Joel to comfort me.

This is one of the manipulation methods of emotional abusers. They refuse to listen or respond to the full weight of the pain that their actions have caused. Why? It touches their insecurity. The walls go up. They don't want to feel that pain. They would rather fight than accept responsibility for your pain. To listen to your feelings and hurt is coming too close to "bonding". To receive the weight of what they have done would crush that "large-fragile" male ego. (Which is otherwise known as "flesh," "self" or "the old nature".)

The "Faith" believer might react like Joel did saying, "I am the righteousness of God. I cannot be touched by those feelings of guilt and shame. What I did is over. The blood has washed me clean and I am guilt free. Now don't bring it up again." This is spiritual abuse. The accomplished spiritual abuser skillfully uses the Word of God to cover his unwillingness to grow and meet his wife's needs. The "breastplate of righteousness" is not to be used to protect you from feeling the consequences of your actions!

A mature believer would realize that his wife is not trying to make him feel guilty or ashamed. She is just trying to share her feelings, which have been crushed by his actions. A mature husband would accept responsibility for her feelings. He would welcome her sharing and comfort her.

A sign of the beginnings of maturity would be if your husband understands that his simple apology does not immediately erase your pain. He has inflicted emotional damage upon you, in some cases for years. A key to his growth into the man that God has called him to be is to accept responsibility for the pain that he has caused you by his abuse, mistreatment or unfaithfulness.

Your husband is growing. He is changing. He is treating you with kindness and showing you sensitivity. He has been doing this now for a total of 48 hours since he has been reading this book! He is now a legend in his own mind! (This is really how guys think!) He has made the decision to be your "knight in shining armor". He is determined to be your dream husband. He is acting and speaking differently.

You are cautious. You tell him that you are wondering if this is real. Is it really is going to last? You are so angry for what he has done and are questioning if he is trying to trick you again. Or is he really sincere?

> **A MATURE HUSBAND WOULD ACCEPT RESPONSIBILITY FOR HER FEELINGS. HE WOULD WELCOME HER SHARING AND COMFORT HER.**

Your husband may react as Joel did! He may be angry that you don't trust him immediately. He has failed the first test. He needs to read *The Man of Her Dreams/The Woman of His!* again! He did not get the message! On the other hand, perhaps he really is getting the message! Perhaps he really **is** going to go all the way with this and become the man of your dreams! You decide to stick your toe into the water and see if this is for real.

In a very nice, feminine and sweet way you might ask him to do something that he formerly would dodge. Perhaps he told you that the request was stupid. In the past he may have yelled at you for this type of request. If he is indeed becoming the husband you need him to be, lo and behold, he does it! You fall out in shock!

Perhaps the next time that he is insensitive to you, you calmly inform him that he has hurt your feelings. Instead of defending himself, your **new husband** says to you, "I'm sorry. I did not mean to hurt your feelings. Thanks for telling me. I will be more careful next time to consider your feelings."

Again, you **crumple** in **utter and complete shock!**

Now you are in a pickle! Do you **trust** him? What do you do? How do you handle **this?** The first and most important thing is that you begin to **respond** to him. **Act** like you have feelings for him. Go out of your way to perform special actions of love toward him. Begin to do things that you know will make him feel happy and comfortable.

If he will continue to change you will slowly find yourself believing that it is **safe** for you to **desire** him again. It is safe to **take those dreams off of the shelf** and begin to fantasize about being married to the man of your dreams because "the heel" is starting to morph into **that man!** Surprise, surprise, surprise! "Wonder of wonders, miracle of miracles! God took a heel and made him a man! Turned him around and miracle of miracles, brought to you a brand new man!" (By the way, that should be sung to the tune of a popular song from the musical "Fiddler on the Roof." It's our attempt at comedy!)

Pretty soon you can unreservedly begin to desire him. This is a good thing. God's plan from the very beginning has been for a wife to desire her husband.

With the fall came a curse: "your husband will **rule** over you." The word "rule" brings to mind the idea of "ruling like a tyrant". It is the Hebrew word, "mashal" meaning "to rule, to have dominion, to have power over." More often than not, when it appears in the Word, it refers to harsh and ungodly rulers. That certainly is the usage of the word in this reference. It was not God's **original intention** that your husband would tyrannize you. It was a result of the curse of the law.

> **A WOMAN'S MISERY WAS THAT THE MAN SHE SO DESIRED WOULD RULE HER LIKE A TYRANT.**

A woman's misery was that the man she so desired would rule her like a tyrant. But this was not God's plan.

By Joel

God's plan is for the new man to reflect His original intention. When we are born again, the carnal man is **supposed** to die and the new man is **supposed** to manifest. Sometimes the **new man** does **not quite make it into a man's home life!** The new man shows up **everywhere else** just **fine!** He can be found in church, at work and in friendships. The **carnal man** waits until he **gets home** to come out!

The carnal man functions as a tyrant over his wife. **The new man functions as a teammate.**

The carnal man demands his way in the same manner that a toddler does. **The new man is gentle and receptive.**

The carnal man is a workaholic, relegating his wife and children to second-class citizenship. They are last on his list! **The new man prioritizes his life with his wife and children. He values them over work, hobbies and church activities.**

The carnal man demands service. **The new man blesses and helps his wife.**

The carnal man has a short, sometimes explosive temper. **The new man is slow to anger, making allowances for shortcomings and mistakes.**

The carnal man is unfaithful. **The new man is devoted to his wife and children.**

The carnal man is uncommunicative and resentful of his wife's efforts at communication. **The new man is open to his wife, engaging in conversation easily.**

The carnal man is despondent when things do not go well. **The new man lives in the joy of the Lord.**

The carnal man is selfish, only being concerned that his needs are met. **The new man looks for ways to meet his family's needs.**

We are teaching your husband to love you as a **redeemed man.** A redeemed man does not rule over his wife. A redeemed man **serves** his wife and **loves her** as Christ loves the church and **gave himself for her** by laying down his life. **A redeemed man is attentive to your needs. A redeemed man dedicates himself to loving his wife and children.**

The curse is reversed! **Your desire is for your husband and he is treating you like the apple of his eye! The better he treats you the more you are safe to unreservedly desire him.**

What is your desired end? You want to feel safe enough to love him **without reservation and never look back.**

Gone are the days of constant bickering, insults, disrespect, humiliation, shame, manipulation and control.

It is a new day — a day of love, fun, freedom, romance and joy!

This new man **is** the man of your dreams.

GOLDEN KEY

DESIRING YOUR HUSBAND WILL ULTIMATELY BRING YOU JOY!

Joel and Kathy,

Your tremendous book is a work of the Holy Spirit... totally inspired by God. Every pastor should have several copies on hand. The more I read of it, the more I continue to stand amazed at the scope of the book's knowledge and wisdom. The Holy Spirit clearly is using you to defend and restore the family, marriage and the church as a whole. Marriage is a most necessary subject that must be addressed in the Body of Christ. Every believer needs help at some point if they want to have a successful marriage.

We continually get reports of believers who are having trouble in their marriage. Our response is to recommend your book. I truly believe that it is the best book on marriage that I have ever read and the most effective, to my knowledge, in producing miracles in these troubled marriages. I will do my part to see that everyone I know has the opportunity to receive a copy.

I am recommending your book to some top-level military chaplains in Iraq whom I am in touch with. The soldiers that they care for desperately need your book. The knowledge it contains could help them successfully resume normal family life upon their return from Iraq. I will also be recommending your book along with other books that I highly esteem in "A Place Called Heaven: Volume 2". I look forward to keeping in touch. You are of a kindred spirit.

Richard Sigmund, D.D., Ph.D., D.O.
Author, "A Place Called Heaven"

<u>*Authors' Note*</u>
Dr. Sigmund is widely known as "Little Richard" from his days as a child who preached in the 1950s tent meetings of Oral Roberts, A.A. Allen, & William Branham. In recent years, his meetings have been marked by miraculous manifestations of the Holy Spirit. His book recounts his visit to heaven while dead for many hours – a "must read."

Chapter Seventeen

Husband, Love Your Wife: Your Lover, Confidant and Friend

Husbands, **love your wives, just as Christ also loved** *the church and gave Himself for her.*
Ephesians 5:25

So husbands ought to **love their own wives** *as their own bodies.*
Ephesians 5:28a

He who **loves his wife** *loves himself. For no one ever hated his own flesh, but nourishes and cherishes it, just as the Lord does the church.*
Ephesians 5:28b-29

Nevertheless let each one of you in particular **so love his own wife as himself.**
Ephesians 5:33a

Husbands, Love your wives.
Colossians 3:19

By Joel

Five times husbands are instructed to love their wives. The Greek word for love here is "agapao" which is the "God kind of love." The GOD KIND OF LOVE expresses itself in **giving** as illustrated in the scriptures: "For God so LOVED the world that He **gave...**" and "Just as Christ also LOVED the church and **gave** himself for her." **You have a high calling, man of God.** That high calling is to love your wife as Christ loves the church and as God loved by **giving** his only son.

This emphasis was revolutionary in the Jewish world 2000 years ago. Women were considered property in their culture. Women were expected to bear and raise children. Husbands were responsible to them in nothing. Husbands could come and go as they pleased with no accountability for where they were or what they had done. **For Paul to demand this level of self-sacrifice from men for their women in that day was nothing short of life altering, conscious shattering and total paradigm shifting!!**

The view that men had of women was shaped by the religion of the day. The disdain that the religious leaders had for women was succinctly illustrated when they dragged the woman caught in adultery out to be stoned while the **man** she had been with was nowhere in sight. His whereabouts were not even mentioned! Even though women had active roles in the Old Testament — Debra the prophetess led God's people to victory in war and Jael killed Sisera — the religion had fallen to a place of total disregard for women.

The prophet Joel had further declared some 1000 years previous that in the last days God would pour out his Spirit on all flesh. This would result in both men and women prophesying. Even with this backdrop, the religious leaders of Jesus' day had relegated women to 2nd class citizenship.

Paul repeatedly told the husbands to lay their lives down for their wives. This was in complete contradiction to the current religious environment. It should be something that we look at seriously. Every husband **can learn** how to love his wife in this way. It is not an **easy thing** to learn! Men are not born with an innate ability to love their wives. It will be a learned ability – an ability that a husband must learn – if he ever hopes to have a relaxed and happy marriage. 1 John 4:19 says, *"We love (Him) because he **first** loved us."* Your job is to love **first**. Your wife's job is to love in **response**.

> **IT IS NOT AN EASY THING TO LEARN! MEN ARE NOT BORN WITH AN INNATE ABILITY TO LOVE THEIR WIVES.**

The first prerequisite understanding of love is that **love is a decision**. It is not based on how you feel. A decision is a decision. It is not a feeling. Kathy and I made it through some very rough years simply because we **decided to love**. We **decided** to stay committed. Kathy, of course, got the short end of the stick, as it was my refusal to listen to her heart that caused our problems. Kathy was operating in "agapao" love. In a marriage relationship, this is above and beyond the call of duty for a wife. When I treated her poorly she **decided** to love me. Many marriage books teach the wife to function in "agapao" love until her husband responds positively to her. Kathy read and applied the message.

This is upside down but sometimes it is the only way a marriage can survive. A man can be so rebellious to meeting his wife's needs that **without** her operating in "agapao" love the marriage would not have a chance to last long enough for the husband to **learn** how to love. This formula **will lengthen** a marriage but will not help a husband to grow into the man that God has called him to be. A man will never **love his wife** in **response** to her "agapao" loving him. He is not **created** to **respond** to his wife. He is created to initiate – to love first – to serve first.

A husband **may** indeed respond **occasionally** to his wife's sacrificing love with warm feelings. **He might buy her flowers and do other acts of love for a time in response to his wife's unconditional love.** This is why the *Total Woman* approach worked in the short-term. A **toddler** will respond to **unconditional love** but when things don't go that child's way they will throw a temper tantrum! Most men approach the emotional issues of marriage at somewhere close to this age. Why? When a child experiences trauma such as divorce, sexual contact or any type of abuse, his emotional growth is arrested. This "arrested development" causes a man to respond emotionally at the same level of maturity that he was at when the trauma stopped his growth.

One of the many benefits of marriage is that God gives this man an opportunity to finish maturing

emotionally. He cannot just have warm feelings for his wife in response to her "perfect submission". He has to learn to hear her heart and meet her needs.

When a wife functions in "agapao" love she enables her husband to stay emotionally immature, continuing in the pattern of abuse. Even an abusive husband will sometimes shower his wife with love; on **his terms.** When he is expressing love on **his** terms his wife is treated well. She gets flowers and gifts! They spend time together! She receives other expressions of love! It's great!

When **she** expresses a need or if she is **mistreated and objects,** suddenly all hell breaks loose. She retreats back into "agapao" love, the storm passes and he selfishly and immediately wants to make love.. Feeling used and abused, she consents in order to keep the peace.

The satisfied husband tells her that he really does not enjoy fighting and he apologizes for "his part" in the fight. He does not define what "his part" was. He leaves that vague. In his reality it was her fault entirely. She gets no closure. He treated her badly and has again escaped taking responsibility for it. She is left "off balance" and unsure of herself. He never lets her get her "equilibrium". At least they are not fighting. He is being kind to her and the cycle begins. This cycle may complete once a month, once a week, twice a week or even every single day!

In the early years of our marriage, I thought in error that **Kathy** was the root of our problems. I made a "heroic" decision to love my flawed wife and stay married to her no matter how badly she acted! It is funny **now! I** was the **hero** for loving **Kathy** (who caused so many arguments in our marriage) when it had been **my** insecurities and pride that hindered me from **meeting her needs.** What a distorted perception of reality I had at the time.

The bottom line to love is that **it is a decision.** I love my spouse **Period.** I **will** act in loving ways. I will **not** entertain the thought of divorce. "Agapao" love emanates from a decision. Jesus did not **feel like** dying on the cross. God did not **feel like** sacrificing His only son. Sometimes you will not **feel like** loving.

> **JESUS DID NOT FEEL LIKE DYING ON THE CROSS. GOD DID NOT FEEL LIKE SACRIFICING HIS SON. SOMETIMES YOU WILL NOT FEEL LIKE LOVING.**

When you met your spouse you were probably infatuated. You fell completely, utterly, madly in love! At least this is how it should have been. Your spouse should have been to you the most wonderful and exciting person in the entire universe.

You thought that your spouse was perfect in every way. Their strengths so overshadowed any potential weaknesses that you knew that you could overlook those weaknesses ("What weaknesses?") and live happily ever after! Your honey validated you, told you how great you were and generated wonderful feelings of self-love and acceptance in you.

If your marriage is like most, at some point you "fell out of love." All of a sudden you did not like each other very much. Suddenly, with just a glance, your spouse could make you feel like you should live under a rock somewhere. One of you now felt superior to the other and that was announced regularly in many ways.

I became a master at manipulating Kathy. If I wanted the house cleaned and did not want to pitch in, I knew exactly how to get her so mad that she would spend two days cleaning the house with all of that energy I stirred up! Her wonderful husband had turned into a master control-freak and manipulator: Dr. Jekyll and Mr. Hyde! The worst part for her was that I could manipulate her so perfectly that I was able to make her look like the bad guy. Everyone in our world who would look into our relationship was convinced that Kathy really had a lot of problems.

Oh, I was really good! You can begin to see what a saint Kathy was when she decided to stand strong and love me by a decision of her will in order to keep our marriage together. Kathy had bought into the teaching that if **she** were **only to submit enough** then **I** would **respond** by becoming a wonderful husband. Though the teaching was ridiculous, it **did** help our marriage to survive long enough for me to get to Colorado and get the education that I needed in order to change.

Who is going to divorce his wife when she is trying to be submissive? Kathy let her man get away with being a heel regularly, cleaned the house when she got mad and never said "no" in bed! Kudos to Kathy!

The upside down "submission" message never helps a husband to grow up and become the man that God has called him to be. It never has and it never will. **Instead** of growing up the man simply has to inform his wife that she is not being submissive. When the heat is turned up he can tell her that she is "rebellious". The Bible declares that rebellion is the same as witchcraft so by playing this card the toddler husband can tell his wife that she is a witch and he has the Bible to prove it!

Our friend Katie said that she replaced the word "submission" with the word, "peacemaker". This was a key God gave her which enabled her to do what was necessary to keep peace in their relationship.

This is a perfect illustration of what Kathy did for me. Kathy waited until I learned how to hear her heart and meet her needs. Thank God for good wives who are able to survive until we husbands finally "get it!" A wife can maintain this position of peacemaker for a season. It is tough. They go with a lot of their needs and desires being unfulfilled, but it is a grace that God gives a wife. She enables her marriage to survive until her husband learns how to be the husband of her dreams!

How did Kathy 'hang in there' for so long. She stood upon the prophetic word that we had received before we were married. ***"You and Kathy will be married and I will touch many through you as a couple."*** Kathy believed God and **received** a miracle! She knew that if she bailed out, the word from God would not come to pass. It is amazing to see the amount of grace

God gives women. They will stay in a bad marriage for years, hoping against hope that things will turn around.

Kathy says, "The failure of our marriage would mark the end of the plan that God had ordained for our life together. It broke my heart to realize that God's dream for us might not come to pass. If we did not succeed, then the course of our life would have been changed forever. I had no intention of accepting this outcome. God had a plan for our family and I was unwilling to accept anything less."

In faith, Kathy loved me with "agapao" love. Her sacrificial love kept us together long enough for the "Colorado Miracle" to happen. In classic God-style, Kathy came to the end of her grace at a time coinciding with our receiving the new information. You are now receiving the truth that will set you free. The days of your wife holding your marriage together are coming to an end. This is your fork in the road. It is our prayer that God will use this book to give to your marriage the same miracle that we received at Colorado! There is no turning back now. Your life can never be the same.

GOLDEN KEY

DECIDE TO LOVE
UNTIL THE MIRACLE HAPPENS.
THEN IT WILL BE EASY.

THOSE PUSHY JEWISH WOMEN!

2000 years ago, Mary said, "Jesus, we are out of wine!" Jesus asked, "What does this have to do with me?" According to Jesus, it was not time to start doing miracles. His mind was made up and He was not budging! Mary ignored Jesus. I can hear her thoughts, "Oh, pardon me, Jesus. I wouldn't want to ask You to do anything! After all, angels sang at Your birth. Wise men traveled many miles to bring You millions of dollars. Hundreds of babies were killed when Herod tried to kill You. You are going to be the savior of the world! You are *only* 30 years old! I wouldn't want to ask You to **do** anything!"

Mary took charge! "Whatever He says to you, do it!" The men who were running the wedding didn't know what to do. Here was a pushy, Jewish/Israeli mother **telling** them what to do. Of course, they obeyed! What else could they do?! His loveable, pushy Jewish mother forced Jesus into performing this first miracle.

Did Jesus rebuke Mary for her lack of submission to the men around her? No. Did He chastise her for embarrassing Him? Jesus? The one and only King of Kings? No. Did He tell her that she was in rebellion or had a Jezebel spirit? No. Jesus did what she demanded. Some would say that Jesus had an Ahab spirit because He let a pushy Middle Eastern woman tell Him what to do!

Flash forward: Jesus is teaching. Martha interrupts the meeting, demanding that Jesus tell Mary to help her. Here is Martha, **another** pushy Israeli woman, telling *Jesus* what to do! Did Jesus rebuke Martha for her "insubordination?" Did Jesus tell Martha that she was operating in witchcraft because she was acting in rebellion to the male leadership in the house? Did He call on the ushers to escort her out because she was out of order? No. Jesus very sweetly said, "Martha, you are very busy. But Mary has chosen the better thing."

Flash Forward: Lazarus is dead. Mary and Martha are upset. "Jesus! If only you had been here, our brother would not have died!" (In other words, "Jesus! It is *your fault* that Lazarus is dead!") Pushy Israeli women! I know a few Israeli women living in Hilton Head Island from a business venture that our family is involved in. I love their personalities. They are strong willed and, yes, they are very, very pushy! We get along great, though. I understand them. In the realm of our business, when they call, I meet their needs, and they are very, very happy! One in particular will call me on the phone saying, "Joel, I need you to come here *today*!" I say, "I am sorry, I am four hours away. I cannot come today." She replies, "No, Joel, you *must* come here *today*. I need you here *today*. You *must* come *today*." So what do I do? I get in the car and drive four hours to "come today!" I have no choice! What else can I do? Pushy, lovable Israeli women!

It was to these pushy, sometimes loud, Israeli/Jewish women that Paul suggested some caution: "Come on ladies, your husbands have to die for you to the same extent that Jesus died for the church. They are going to do anything that you ask of them. They are laying down their lives for you. Five times I have told them that they have to love you with 'agape' love. This means that they have to lay their lives down for you, regardless of what you do, and expect nothing in return. I have not told you to love your husbands with 'agape' love one single time. That is not your job. You are only asked to respond warmly and lovingly with 'phileo' love to your husbands as they lay their lives down for you. Please don't take advantage of your husbands. They are at your mercy. You Israeli women can be very pushy, so while your husbands die for you, meet your needs and adapt/submit to you, be sure that you also adapt/submit to them!"

"Hupotasso." "Subordinate." "Hupotasso" to *one another*, husbands and wives. It is *a key* to marriage success. But, men, listen to me and listen to me very clearly. NEVER, NEVER, NEVER tell your wife that she has to submit to you because you are the head of the house. When you one day realize what a huge insult this is to the death that Jesus died for His bride, you will feel great grief for so belittling His sacrifice. You are to lay your life down for her as Christ did for you.

Pastors and teachers, quit telling women that if they will "just submit to their husbands" that they will have a successful marriage. It *does not work* that way. Take this pressure off of the wives. The success of a marriage is *not* dependent on a man's wife. Women are not *required* nor are they *equipped* by God to carry this load. Teach men to lay their lives down for and serve their wives. When husbands deal with *their own* issues, the wives will do fine. In 99.9% of cases, the wives are not the **root** nor are they the **solution** to the marriage problems. When a husband gets right, his "wife issues" will often magically disappear. If men receive this paradigm, you will have happy marriages, which equals happy men and very, very happy women.

Thanks so much, Joel and Kathy!

FYI… My Jay is a CHANGED MAN because of this book!

Lisa, Michigan

<u>*Authors' Note*</u>
Jay is a prophet who ministers internationally and is also in our area on a regular basis. According to his testimony, when we gave Jay a copy of "The Man of Her Dreams/The Woman of His!" his attention was riveted. Jay read over 100 pages on the flight from Florida to Michigan. Lisa had not even read the book yet when she began to remark favorably to some friends about how much the book had blessed their marriage. Jay was surprised when a friend asked him if they could get a copy of the book that Lisa said had so greatly enhanced their marriage! Jay said, "Lisa has not even read it yet. How does she know it is good?" The friend replied that Lisa was bragging about how wonderful Jay had been since reading the book!

Since that time, Jay has introduced the book in Hawaii, Australia, Africa and in various other states in the USA. Jay shared the following testimony recently at a local church in Daytona Beach. Two women, one in Africa and the second one in Australia, happily reported that their husbands said, "I love you" to them for the first time in forty years… within two hours of the book entering their homes. Two separate couples. Two different nations. One common heartbreak of forty years. The first light at the end of the tunnel came because of Jay sharing a simple life-changing book.

Attention pastors, prophets, evangelists, lay ministers and traveling teachers: You have an opportunity. You can add this book to your ministry by purchasing it in high quantities and offering it everywhere you go. Your effort will bring miracles to many marriages.

Chapter Eighteen

Fond of Man
And Affectionate

Teach them to love their husbands.
Titus 2:4

By Kathy

In the first chapter of the Bible, God revealed that it is His plan and design for women to desire their husbands. This has been God's way from the beginning.

*Your **desire** shall be for your husband.*
Genesis 3:16

We share keys that encourage men to love their wives and encourage women to positively respond to their husbands with a natural, affectionate fondness. This is the formula for successful marriage.

We want men to become the husbands that their wives need them to be so that their wives will feel safe to open-heartedly love their husbands in response.

When a woman feels safe, the desire that God put in her for a great relationship with her husband can operate unhindered. The husband then reaps the benefit of having a wife who feels safe, secure and loved.

In Chapter 17 we studied the principle of a husband loving his wife. If a husband is to love his wife with "agapao" love, how is the wife supposed to love?

There is only one **specific** verse telling wives to love their husbands.

Teach them to love their husbands.
Titus 2:4

This word for "love" in Greek is "philandros" and it means "fond of man and affectionate." It is a responsive love. We encourage women to respond to their husbands by being fond and affectionate.

> **IF YOU TREAT YOUR WIFE LIKE A QUEEN SHE'LL BE HAPPY TO DO THINGS FOR YOU!**

Once, Joel and I were in a convenience store making a purchase. Joel forgot his wallet in the car and asked me if I would go out to the car and get it for him. I said, "Yes, sir!" and turned to go out the door.

With complete and utter astonishment a young man exclaimed to Joel, "How did you do that?" Joel said, "How did I do what?" He said, "That! How did you get her to say 'Yes, sir' and go get your wallet just like that?"

Joel replied, "I treat her like a queen! If you treat your wife like a queen she'll be **happy** to do things for you!"

Isn't that how you are?

When your husband is treating you wonderfully, it is easy to be a blessing to him, isn't it?

If your husband only realized how much more enjoyable life will be when he finally begins to listen to your heart and treat you like a queen he would certainly become that husband that you need him to be a lot quicker!

If an excellent wife had to choose between living with a less intelligent, less successful man who treated her well or a successful, more intelligent man who treated her poorly, she would choose the former every time.

Brains and success don't hold a candle to gentleness and kindness to an excellent wife. She would live in a shack with a man who treats her right! Fortunately, you do not have to make that choice! Your husband can be intelligent, successful and yes, he can learn to treat you right!

When your man lays his life down for you and meets your needs then you are enabled to respond by being fond of and affectionate toward him in return.

This is extremely easy to do if you have not been too humiliated, broken and confused by your husband's actions of the past. If you **have** been humiliated and broken it will take time for you to heal and trust again. You might have retreated into a protective shell and may be wary of opening your heart.

You may be afraid to take the risk.
Why be hurt again?

If your relationship has been damaged to **this** extent, your husband will have to display that he is sincere over an extended period. **In time** you will trust that it is safe for you to come out of hiding. **In time** you will respond positively to him.

You **are able** to be the wife of his dreams and you **will be** in response to him becoming the husband that you need him to be. Are you ready to be his dream wife **today?** No. **Today** you want **nothing** to **do** with him.

What is his answer? The answer is for your husband to love, love, and love you with that "agapao" love without expecting anything in return.

When we meet a wife who has **no desire** for her husband there are always years of history that killed that response. It is doubtful that **any** woman married a man without having the desire for a great relationship with him!

No woman, who has a choice, willingly gets married thinking, "I don't like this guy. He is an idiot. I don't want to be with him. I certainly don't like romance with him. He is a total heel. However, I will get married to him, sleep with him, make babies and let him pay the bills."

Women do not think this way. Even in cultures that have arranged marriages, we dream. We dream in terms of ideals, fantasies and excitement. We may not get what we dreamed of, but we dream! Even a husband in an arranged marriage can fulfill those dreams. If you are the husband in an arranged marriage, who just happens to be reading this chapter, it is true: you **can** learn to fulfill your wife's dreams… and ultimately, yours!

If ten years into marriage a wife has no interest in her husband or in their relationship, there invariably have been years of failure on his part to be the husband his wife has needed him to be.

This couple has a challenge.

1. He must convince his wife by actions that he is changing.

2. She at some point has to accept this possibility in good faith and open her heart. This could take days, weeks, months or years depending on the severity of the damage and his sincerity in changing. At some point she will have to allow the good feelings to flow again.

3. He has to continue to grow and change as she shares her heart

This is where it usually breaks down. Most men have large and fragile egos. They tend to fight and resist every suggestion that their wife makes! God really had a sense of humor when he combined large and fragile into one male ego! What a useless combination!

We know of a pastor who was extremely physically abusive to his wife. He did not wake up until his wife left him and got a restraining order against him.

God taught him the principles that changed his life and he wanted to make it right with her.

For two years, he fulfilled his child support responsibilities, gave her additional money, cut her grass and bought groceries for her, secretly leaving them on her doorstep.

> **IF A WIFE HAS NO INTEREST IN HER HUSBAND, THERE INVARIABLY HAVE BEEN YEARS OF FAILURE ON HIS PART TO BE THE HUSBAND HIS WIFE NEEDED HIM**

For the first few months she would not even talk to him. He persisted in his actions of love. He had decided that his only course of action was to dedicate the rest of his life to making up to his wife for all of the abuse that she had endured. He committed himself to this task whether she ever responded to him or not. Two years later they were remarried.

This is "agapao" love, the God kind of love that requires no response. Selfish love, on the other hand, puts forth some effort and then **demands** a response.

A great starting place for a marriage relationship that is growing yet in need of repair would be this:

1. Both husband and wife operate in "agapao" love. We ask this of a wife who has reached the point of believing her husband **sincerely wants to grow and change.** He will fail at times. He will make mistakes and revert to his old patterns at times.

   If she believes that he is sincere, she can make allowance for mistakes. This will lift a little pressure off of him.

   We do not endorse a woman sitting back with a stubborn attitude saying to herself, "After he changes I will respond."

   If you have **decided** you are married **permanently** and **love out of a decision** you will attempt to lighten his load in learning to love you.

2. The wife is free to communicate her frustrations to her husband and he listens to her heart and changes. The husband cannot tell her why her needs are invalid. He has to validate and legitimize her thoughts and feelings.

3. As he becomes the husband his wife needs him to be, she begins to freely respond with fondness and affection. She makes a decision to respond to him with that "philandros" love as the Bible instructs, meaning to be "fond of man and affectionate."

4. When the husband has grown to the point that his wife is his first priority and he is meeting her needs then she naturally begins to express the fond,

affectionate love that comes out of having a desire for her husband. It is no longer an effort. She easily loves with "philandros" love. She is truly becoming "fond of (her) man and affectionate."

At some point hereafter the relationship goes into "overdrive".

The feelings flow. You fall in love again.

You would rather be with your sweetheart than anyone else even though you do enjoy other wholesome friendships.

You naturally meet each other's needs. You are a team and you communicate constantly as a natural course of events.

You build each other up when one of you is down, you anticipate each other's needs and you lighten each other's load.

You are on the same page in life, love and play.

You respect each other as individuals and celebrate your differences.

You play together, love together and laugh together.

You are best friends, lovers, confidants and team members.

You are each coach **and** team member!

You are one flesh. You have one heart!

You can say that you are more in love today than you have ever been.

Joel and I have this relationship today. If Joel and Kathy can do it, you can too!

No matter what you have been through, there is hope!

Today is the first day of the rest of your life.

The rest of your life is the best of your life.

Take a risk.

GOLDEN KEY

TAKE A RISK TODAY!
RESPOND POSITIVELY AND WARMLY
TO YOUR HUSBAND'S EFFORTS

Hi Joel and Kathy,

I was married for 25 years to a Bible College director and associate pastor of a big church in Fort Worth. We got a divorce a number of years ago because he had several affairs with students. He was a workaholic who never came home (taught day and night classes). I was a Bible College instructor and Christian journalist (editor of a 500,000 circulation Christian newspaper in Dallas). I worked two ministry jobs but was at home at night to raise my sons.

My ex sounds exactly like Joel and I'll bet there are many more preachers who need your book. I didn't want to cause my husband more problems than he already had. I didn't discuss his problems or ours with anyone and he expected me to work out anything bothering me with God alone.

He continually inflicted guilt on me, besides the other abuses. I wanted my marriage restored but I wanted him to come clean on his own and tell the senior pastor. (I felt he would resent me more if I did and things would never be healed.) I wouldn't go above his head. I was wrong in protecting him, but at the time I didn't believe I was... I thought I was acting out of love. In reality I was enabling him to keep his lousy attitude, bad morals and continue his pattern of hurting other people.

I admire you, Kathy and Joel, for having the fortitude and humble hearts to tell your story honestly with such transparency. God will use you to help restore thousands of Christian homes and to teach others to build a Christian marriage. I lived in a private pain without telling anyone for years while we were in ministry. That was wrong and that is my final conclusion.

Dr. L. D. Kramer gave me your book. He had ministered to Paul Hegstrom when he was still abusive. I read it cover to cover that very night. It is as if Joel's experience was exactly like my ex-husband. I prayed for *him through ten years of unfaithfulness and covered his sin for so long. I grew tired of lying about our rotten personal life.*

As it turned out, the senior pastor of our church was not interested in the truth. When he did find out about the adultery, he was more concerned about discrediting me and hoping to keep my mouth shut. He kept my husband in the pulpit and privately put him on guilt trips. He handled the entire thing so poorly that he even paid the legal bills for my ex to secure a divorce as quietly as possible.

My ex didn't want custody of our children but the pastor told him that he had to fight to get them if he wanted to keep his job. If he lost the children, he would look like the guilty one. It was unbelievable what my husband did to keep his pride intact.

My ex, with the help of the senior pastor, filed a counter suit. I wouldn't agree to anything but joint custody. Finally, I had to threaten to bring the adultery out into the open simply to get them to agree to joint custody. They backed off and we settled, but they still publicly smeared my ministry and me. My children heard all kinds of things about me at their church and school that weren't true.

The truth won out, though. My children ultimately realized that I was not the bad guy!

My oldest son is 24 and wants to get married this year. He is pure hearted, but he graduated from his dad's school and I am concerned he has developed many of the same attitudes. (If so, he is not ready for marriage.) I believe that if he heard Joel's perspective he would be tender enough before God to adjust those attitudes and misconceptions about marriage before they hinder his relationship.

Abuse is a cycle that must be broken in families. Young people need this book before they get married. Families are dysfunctional in relationships and children learn from their parents. I don't want my kids to go through the heartache of something when they can learn from the experiences of others instead.

I've already recommended your book to about 25 couples and I've only had it since Tuesday! Thank you for your obedience to God's call and for being so graphically honest. It's real, pure and life changing.

I will recommend this to a Christian psychologist who will love it. She did marriage counseling with my ex and me. My husband only showed up for one full session and one half session. The psychologist totally had him pegged. He was too arrogant to believe that he needed help. I went to all the sessions and God changed me and helped me heal.

Eventually truth will be revealed. God promotes in His time. God is stronger than the garbage we face. I am remarried now, totally blessed and happy. I'm again working full-time in the ministry, writing and teaching at a Bible College.

In those first 25 years of ministry and marriage, I ministered in 24 countries, built an international Christian newspaper and taught all over the world for 18 years with signs and wonders following. The past three years of my new marriage have been more wonderful than anything that I experienced in those 25 years combined.

I have a wonderful relationship with my sons and the most wonderful husband on earth. Life is a joy. I am on the ground floor of starting new Christian publications, writing books and Christian college curriculum and I'm about to help start three new Bible schools. The devil can knock you down, but he can't knock you out!

Every couple that reads your book and takes it to heart will be blessed. Your powerful testimony should always be told. Thank you for your obedience to God. Many, many, many marriages will be saved. I'm sure of that.

Blessings,

Rosanna Logan

Chapter Nineteen

If It Doesn't Work At Home, Don't Export It.
(For Ministers)

For an Elder must be a man whose life cannot be spoken against. **He must be faithful to his wife.**

1 Timothy 3:2 (NLT)

By Joel

Many couples reading this book **are now** or **will be** called into ministry. The enemy loves to cause marital failure and he takes **special delight** in making a **public display** of his deceptive abilities by putting additional pressure on the marriages of those who are called to ministry.

If a man cannot meet the needs of his own wife, then he **cannot** meet the needs of families in the household of God. A man's first priority in ministry must be to be faithful to his wife physically, spiritually and emotionally.

Ministers are tempted to get their needs met through church work. The enemy of their marriage wants them to spend their best energies on church and on church members. In many ministry environments, ministers' wives are left on the outside looking in.

I remember being told by the "soon departing" elders of our second pastorate that Kathy was not allowed to participate in the elders' meetings. That policy was changed immediately!

Excluded ministry wives sit quietly in the pew watching their husbands getting "oohs" and "ahs" from admiring ministry supporters or congregation members. It is easy for this minister to be unfaithful to his wife by drawing his self-image and self-worth from those in his congregation.

This is a form of emotional adultery.

These longsuffering ministers' wives die inside knowing full well that their husbands are not meeting their needs and not living the life in private that they are attempting to display in public.

When the wife complains, the husband tells her that ministry is his most important call and that she is being rebellious to God to suggest that he slow down in his ministry. This is spiritual abuse.

Many times these relationships continue in misery for years behind closed doors. When one of these wives gets the nerve up to leave, they are ostracized from the church body. The official word from the leadership is that the wife is in rebellion.

The reality is that the husband is in spiritual and emotional adultery, having neglected his marital responsibilities under the guise of ministry commitment. Ministry is his mistress.

A pastor in Central Florida recently continued to lead his church of thousands while separated from his wife. He maintained this position of leadership and influence all the way through to the completion of the divorce. I predict that he will be introducing a new and improved wife within a year or two. Because of his influence, the divorce rate will skyrocket in that church body.

> SADLY ENOUGH, MANY CHURCH MEMBERS ALSO STAY LOYAL TO THE MAN. THIS CONTRIBUTES TO THE DESTRUCTION OF THE MARRIAGE.

He has acted like so many others with whom Satan has had his way. These men stay in the pulpit, resentful of any suggestion that they step out of ministry. Instead of forsaking the ministry to pursue meeting their wife's needs they cling to their position of authority, stubborn and defiant.

Sadly enough, many church members also stay loyal to the man. This contributes to the destruction of the marriage. Their loyalty enables the husband to have his emotional needs fulfilled by ministry commitments and activity. Our hearts break over the tragedy of these public ministry divorces. Pray for those involved. Pray that their marriages be restored. But don't attend their church.

We understand the manipulation and control to which these wives have been subjected behind closed doors. I know what it means to step out of ministry and go through the painful growth needed to become the man that God has called me to be by becoming the husband that my wife needs me to be.

The temptation that ministers face at this point is to stay in their pulpit or at the helm of their ministry. The enemy of their souls suggests to them that they should just keep on ministering without missing a beat.

The point is **not** that a pastor's wife left him. The **point** is that his wife's departure was a **cumulative response to years of manipulation, neglect, abuse and control.** This was **not** a **sudden** decision.

I tell my congregation regularly, "If Kathy ever leaves me and she is gone for more than three weeks, then I want you to leave my church. If I have not set things right, do not enable me to stay in the pulpit.

"It does not matter **what I say** to justify myself and vilify Kathy. It does not matter **how much** I beg you to stay. Your responsibility would be to leave my church or ministry so that I have no choice but to pursue restoration with the wife of my youth."

When our marriage was in crisis, I desperately wanted to stay in the pulpit! My thoughts were along the following lines:

"It is not **all** my fault. Divisive church members caused our congregation to go through a messy church split. Kathy was causing me problems. Besides, I came back! I repented! Everyone should just accept me and validate my immediately continuing in public ministry."

If someone could have looked into our lives at the time they would have seen the truth that Kathy and I were fighting a lot.

I was insisting that we still be friends with the other couple. They agreed. This development put a knife through Kathy's heart. I was still infatuated, in false love or in lust with the other woman. Pick whatever term you want to use to describe it.

> **WHEN OUR MARRIAGE WAS IN CRISIS, I DESPERATELY WANTED TO STAY IN THE PULPIT.**

The relationship was broken but there was still a strong soul tie. I had a difficult time letting God circumcise my heart.

Thank God that my character flaws forced me to face the fact that I had to step out of the pulpit for a season to restore my family. Why other ministers sometimes do not realize this, I will never know. It is total and complete deception.

Situations like this have become very ugly in the "Full Gospel" segment of the Body of Christ.

A well-known, successful young pastor in California divorced his wife and then remarried in 3 weeks to a new and improved wife. A famous bishop from Georgia officiated while the young minister stayed in the pulpit without missing a beat.

It saddens me to witness the enemy succeeding in his goal of destroying not just one minister and his family with adultery, but two. In this case the bishop joined himself to this man's sin and both of them fell because of the same deception.

Adultery takes months to develop. It is never like, "Oops! I just woke up in her bed. I have no idea how it happened. Oh well, just forgive me and accept me." No, this type of sin takes years to develop. You don't just get over the damage and mindset by getting remarried or by taking a few months' sabbatical!

One of the pioneers of marriage ministry who had a huge influence on the Body of Christ in the 1970's and 1980's recently divorced his wife and married a younger woman. His comment was this: "The principles that I taught were good. I just did not live them." To his credit, he at least ended his ministry and voluntarily disappeared.

My heart was free from the soul tie after a year or so. About that time, I heard that a pastor we know had gotten into adultery. He had been our pastor in the early 1980s when we lived in Ohio. Pastor Ross had a very even temperament. He was not as exciting and emotional as I was. He was a slow and steady "plodder". I appreciated his secure influence as I went out during the week to slay giants!

Pastor Ross steadily taught the Word of God. The church grew from 10 people to a strong body of 200 committed believers in a few years. Everyone loved his relaxed and matter-of-fact presentation of the Word.

Mrs. Ross was a beautiful and excellent pastor's wife. There is no other way to describe her. I recall the appreciation service for Pastor Ross at which Mrs. Ross announced that she, like Sarah, was not ashamed to call her husband "lord". They appeared to have a wonderful flow of the Spirit, a talented praise team, volunteers staffing the nursery, children and youth ministries... everything looked wonderful.

When I heard about his fall I was shocked. I had been out of touch with him for a number of years but we had gone to services when we were in town visiting Kathy's parents. Everything appeared to be fine. Pastor Ross was the last person who I would ever have expected to be in this situation.

I called Pastor Ross as soon as I heard the bad news. It had been one month; he was back with his family. I wanted to encourage him in what I felt at the time was the most important aspect of his recovery. I said, "The most important thing that I can tell you is to be sure that you let God circumcise your heart completely. I struggled with a soul tie for almost two years and that really hurt Kathy. For some reason I could not bring myself to make a break in my heart. You have a more steady personality than I do so hopefully you will be able to immediately break that thing." Pastor Ross assured me that he had already circumcised his heart. I was glad for him.

About one year later we ran into one of the church members at an amusement park. To my inquiry as to the health of the church, we were informed that Pastor Ross had left his wife and was now married to the other woman. That was a great disappointment. He had not circumcised his heart after all.

Had we **understood** the principles **then** that we have shared in *The Man of Her Dreams/The Woman of His!* we could have helped him more. This all happened **before** we went to Colorado. We were struggling just to survive!

The challenge for your marriage is this: **Live** the **Word. Stay faithful** to your wife by **putting her first in everything.** If you find that you are not having a successful marriage then you **should not be exporting what you are living.** You know what is going on behind the closed doors of your home. Are you manipulating and devaluing your wife? Is your home a battleground? If so, recognize the problem and fix it. Get some serious counseling. Don't wait until your wife leaves you.

In the early 90's, one of my favorite ministers was brought down by financial accusations, most of which turned out to be false. His former wife now shares how my "hero of the faith" had walked away from his marital responsibilities **long** before the false accusations publicly brought his ministry down.

Another "hero of the faith" to me was the premier promoter of daily prayer. He also divorced in the 1990's. It turns out that he had been bipolar. His ex-wife believes that if he had been diagnosed earlier and utilized the prescribed medication, they may have never divorced.

These were two of my favorite "heroes of the faith" in my formative and early years of public ministry. **Who is safe?** He who judges himself honestly and **stays accountable to his wife** is safe! After all, she is the person who knows him best!

> **HE WHO JUDGES HIMSELF HONESTLY AND STAYS ACCOUNTABLE TO HIS WIFE IS SAFE!**

"Who, me? Be accountable - to my wife? There is **no way! She** is supposed to **submit to me!"** Okay! **Don't** grow up! **Stay** a child! **Create misery** in your home!

These are spectacular examples. What I am more concerned about is what is going on behind closed doors in **your** home. Do **you** love **your** wife as **Christ** loved the **church** by **laying your life down** for her and meeting her needs as she expresses them?

On the other hand, could you be spiritually and emotionally abusing her while committing spiritual and emotional adultery with your ministry supporters?

- Do you tell people that your wife is in rebellion?

- Do you say that she might have a Jezebel spirit?

225

- Do you harp on your wife that she has to "submit to you" and remember that you are the "head of the house?"

If your answer is **"yes"** to **any** of these questions, you are in need of some serious marriage counsel. Deal with it! Don't hide!

I have openly shared how I mistreated Kathy in all of the above and in many other ways. God has given us supernatural amnesia to not remember all of the individual instances. If it were not for that amnesia we could fill a 1,000-page book describing our experiences.

Our hearts' desire is that *The Man of Her Dreams/The Woman of His!* would help many ministry marriages that are abusive and/or are recovering from adultery. We have asked the Holy Spirit to bring to mind the illustrations that He wanted us to share. If you found yourself in even one illustration and have been helped, we are grateful. Our transparency is being used by God to reach, to touch and to heal.

We would have written this book in the 90's but we had to walk it out. We had to successfully live these principles for a long time before we could share them in writing.

We can now say without a moment's hesitation:

"The principles that have now given us **our** dream marriage can save **any** marriage. If a husband and wife **utilize** these principles, **any marriage** can be turned around. The **worst marriage** can become a **dream marriage.** The **most abusive** husband **can** become 'The Man of Her Dreams'. The **wife** who has been **hurt the most can** become 'The Woman of His'. If we can do it, so can you."

You can do this. You, man of God, can grow up. You can lay your life down for your wife. You can listen to the Personal Marriage Manual that God has given you in your wife. You can be kind, sensitive, gentle, loving and supportive.

If you will do this, your wife will respond. She will do and become anything that you want her to do and become. God made her that way. She will respond to you. Your job is to be the husband she needs you to be.

Remember to always put your wife's need for time, attention and support above the needs of your congregation or ministry supporters. You will end up having a great marriage relationship and **that** will be something that you can export!

GOLDEN KEY

YOUR MARRIAGE IS
ALWAYS FIRST PRIORITY

BE YOUR OWN HERO

You have come to the end of this exciting journey of discovery. For what might be a first, you have the tools that can enable you to experience an outrageously happy marriage. If you "work the program," arguing will be a thing of the past. Misunderstandings will vanish. Strife will no longer be master in your home.

Wives, we have empowered you and set you free. You don't have to suffer in silence anymore. Your husband is open to your input. He is willing to listen to your heart. You are free to speak, free to express yourself. Your man can be your hero. We have given him the tools. All that he has to do is work them.

*Husbands, we have given you the keys that you need to become the man that God has called you to be. When you have mastered these keys, you will find that your wife will begin to transform into the wife that you always dreamed of having. Not because she **has** to. She will fulfill your dreams because she **wants** to, because she **knows** that you love her; she **feels** that you love her. **If you live this life successfully, you will be your own hero. How great is that?***

Our hearts break when we consider the many well-known ministers who were not living the heroic lives that we imagined. Time and time again, we hear of yet another of our "heroes of the faith" who have been unfaithful, whose marriages have failed, or who have fallen into other major sin. As new reports surface, almost daily it seems, we realize how insidious the enemy is. Yes, there are national leaders that are setting wonderful examples, but the list grows shorter every day. This breaks our hearts.

The only solution to this problem is obvious. We must live the life that we once believed our heroes were living. We must be our own heroes. You must be your own hero. If you have a happy marriage with your wife, if you love the Lord with all of your heart, mind and strength, if you spend time in the Word and prayer every day, if you treat your children well and love unsaved people, if you are faithful at church, if you balance time between your spouse, your children, your church and your work, you are our heroes. You are your own hero.

Many years ago, Prophet George Moss prophesied to us: "You will not be able to look to the right or to the left, for this hand held out, or that hand held out, but as it comes, you will know that it comes from Me." We never understood what that word from God meant. Now we know. Most of our heroes are gone. We are living the life that we thought they were living. We have become our own heroes. It is a new day. God is raising up a new breed of heroes who are spiritually healthy. Heroes who have good marriages. An army of heroes. Everyday heroes. You have the tools. Live this life. Be your own hero. Starting today.

Chapter Twenty

Turn The Heat Up!
(For Adults Only)

Let each man **have his own wife** *and let each woman* **have her own husband.**
1 Corinthians 7:2b

By Joel and Kathy

We do not ascribe to the religiously correct concept that sex is "not all that important" in a marriage. We think that it is **very** important and it is clear that the **Bible** gives lovemaking a place of **high importance** in a married couple's life!

Our intention is **not** to cover the full scope of making love in sixteen pages! There are many Christian books that are fully dedicated to this subject. We recommend *Sheet Music* by Dr. Kevin Leman, *The Act of Marriage* by Tim and Beverly LaHaye and *Intimate Issues* by Linda Dillow and Lorraine Pintus. We just want to shake a few branches and loosen things up!

I heard Zig Ziglar say this, "Have you heard it taught that a man becomes what he thinks about all day long? I have to disagree. If that premise were true, then every teenage boy would be a *woman!*" A husband is not depraved because he thinks about making love... all the time. This is why God created "multi-tasking".

It is important to remember that bedroom delight starts in the morning and builds throughout the day. If a husband is changing into the man that God has called him to be, then wonderful things are happening. He is becoming more sensitive, gentle and kind. He is not resisting when his wife mentions that he hurt her feelings or did something in an uncaring way.

If a husband treats his wife special all day long, calling her from work to say "Hi", opening car doors, offering attention and hugs, then the bedroom temperature will rise pleasantly all day long! Someone once said that a woman is like a crock-pot and a man is like a microwave. It does not turn me on to think of Kathy as a crock-pot (how sexy is a crock-pot?), but I have learned to honor the crock-pot theory. All day long is an adventure for Kathy and me!

When it comes time to retire for the evening, don't lose the pleasant mood that has been building! Go to bed at the same time! If you are a night owl then get back up when your partner goes to sleep. A good aim would be to go to bed at the same time at least five nights a week. That is minimum. It is not possible to stay close as a married couple if you go to bed at different times every night.

A woman is not designed to carry a sexual load without an emotional reward and a man is not designed to carry an emotional load without a sexual reward. This is part of God's design and plan. Husband, if you meet your wife's emotional needs, she will be more than happy to meet your sexual needs. Sometimes it is a challenge for you to be sensitive and meet your wife's emotional needs and sometimes it is difficult for your wife to be excited about meeting your sexual needs. The more that you meet her emotional needs in the kitchen, living room and dining room, though, the more excited and eager to please she will be in the bedroom; as a response to you becoming more Christlike.

> *May your fountain be blessed and may you rejoice in the wife of your youth. May her breasts satisfy you always, may you ever be captivated by her love.*
> *Proverbs 5:18-19*

GUYS, DON'T EXPECT HER TO TURN INTO A SEX GODDESS EVERY TIME YOU ARE FRISKY. SOMETIMES IT TAKES ALL THAT SHE HAS JUST TO BE AVAILABLE.

If a couple makes love whenever **one** of the partners is interested then your marriage will include **lots** of lovemaking! This is a valid goal for every marriage! Guys are normally more interested in **quantity** and gals are more interested in the **quality.** If you make love **often,** most husbands will be happy with the love life. If you enjoy quality **time** together, most wives will be happy.

What do we recommend? Lots of sex! Lots of variety! Have lovemaking "dates" at times other than right before bedtime. Afternoon and mid-morning delights are great as you have more energy than you do at midnight! **There is no such thing as too much lovemaking or too much time** spent at any one time!

If you are interested and your spouse is not, then go for a "quickie". Some guys are more than happy to have a "quickie" a few times a week. An excellent wife will be happy to meet his needs even if she is ready to go to sleep! Ladies, do not let your man go to bed wanting! Guys, don't expect her to turn into a "sex goddess" every time you are frisky. Sometimes it takes all that she has just to be available!

Words of caution to a husband who is recovering from being a control-freak:

- It is a turn off for most women to participate in any form of lovemaking if her husband is not clean! Take a shower!

- If your wife is hesitant, do not force it. Talk the issues through. Pray together. Let the principles of gentleness and loving kindness guide you.

- If you have children, you cannot have your wife until you have helped with the many demands that come with a busy family: helping children with homework, cleaning dishes, folding laundry, etc.

- In other words, you must **first do** whatever **you** can do **in general** to enable your wife to have an enjoyable and relaxing evening. **Don't relax in the bedroom waiting.** Don't sit around watching TV or going for joy ride to pass the time while your wife helps the kids with the homework, does the dishes and chases after the baby!

- If this subject is causing problems between you, purchase and read *Sheet Music* together! Drop the subject until you have done this.

It came as a surprise to us to find out that Christian couples can have so many various hang-ups about making love. Some unfortunate couples will argue about what **is** and what **is not** acceptable. Then there is the **time, place, length** and **intensity** of the lovemaking to argue about. Afterward, they can argue over who **is** and is **not** contributing enough energy and zest at any given time. Egads! Lovemaking should be the easiest part of married life! After all, it is really, really fun if done right!

God designed lovemaking to be fun! There are many "right" ways! Not everyone has this attitude. Scott would get bothered when he wanted to make love and his wife was tired or uninterested. She would be agreeable to meeting his needs but this was not enough for Scott.

His feelings would get hurt because she did not use the right tone of voice. He would push her to get into the mood when she was not "going there" until he frustrated himself **so much** that he would get up and leave the room! Then he would **complain** that they were not making love often enough! Scott took it as a personal insult if his wife and mother of four active children did not respond exactly as he envisioned her doing in his perfectionist ideal world. As Charles Capps would say, "This is ignorance gone to seed!" **Get over it!** Your wife does not have to be a sex goddess every night. Sometimes she is tired. Sometimes she is stressed.

The Man Of Her Dreams/
The Woman Of His!

Sue and Andy had the opposite problem. Sue resented Andy if he knew that she was tired and he still wanted a quickie. Sue, like Scott in the previous example, thought that she and Andy should only make love when they were both interested and had plenty of energy. Sue wanted everything perfect, expressing that she felt used when Andy wanted to have a nightcap. **Get over it!** Neither spouse should demand perfect sex every time.

There are so many other potential arguments in a marriage. How can something that God created to be as fun as sex be turned into occasion to argue? The intimate physical union of a man and woman was God's crowning creation! He designed it for procreation, sure! We do not object to that! We have four children and a couple in Heaven from miscarriages! In addition to procreation, making love is also the ultimate gift from our Heavenly Father! His gift enables a husband and wife to give the greatest pleasures to one another and just plain have fun! Let's enjoy God's generosity a little bit! If you must argue about something, pick another topic!

Let the husband **render to his wife the affection** *due her, and also likewise* **the wife to her husband.**

The **wife does not have authority** *over her own* **body** *but* **the husband does.** *And likewise* **the husband does not have authority** *over his own* **body** *but* **the wife does. Do not** *deprive one another.*
1 Corinthians 7:2b – 5a

You could emphasize this passage in ten different ways arriving at ten different and interesting conclusions every time! If Kathy and I were to paraphrase this passage, it would read like this:

"When a husband wants to make love, his wife should say, 'Let's go for it!' When a wife wants to make love, the husband should say, 'Let's go for it!'" A husband should show his wife lots of affection and attention whenever she is interested and his wife should be ready to give him attention and affection when he is interested."

"The wife does not get to tell her husband 'No!' She does not have authority over her body. If he wants it, he gets it! The husband does not get to say 'No' when his wife is interested, either! If she wants his body, she gets it! **She** is in charge of **his** body and **he** is in charge of **hers!** A man or woman should not ever hold back or be resistant, rather they are to be eager and excited participants!" This is pretty straightforward talk from the Word of God concerning a married couple's private life!

> ***Marriage*** *is* **honorable** *among* **all** *and* **the bed undefiled...**
> *Hebrews 13:4a*

If we were to paraphrase this verse we would say: "Everyone agrees that being married is honorable. The best part is that when you are married your sex life gets to be full of variety, excitement, fun and adventure!" How fun can the private life be for a married Christian couple in the light of these verses? Lots of fun! Rick Godwin pointed out on national television years ago that there are no verses in the Bible telling you that certain sexual positions or acts are wrong. As long as the sex involves only you and your spouse, anything goes! Were we ever glad to hear that from a nationally known and highly esteemed minister of the Gospel!

We are often asked what we believe is acceptable sex according to the Word of God. Our reply is simple and direct. "Anything that you and your spouse want to do that is mutually agreeable and does not cause physical harm is fine. The Bible says that the marriage bed is undefiled."

In *Intimate Issues,* which we purchased from Focus on the Family, the authors point out that anything between a husband and wife is acceptable, unless it is obvious sin. If either partner wants to have sex that includes other people, X-rated videos or pornography of any kind, this is very simply sin. Sex is designed to be between a husband and wife... **only**. There are to be no partners, even if they are on a TV screen, in a magazine or via the Internet. When a man partakes of pornography, he brings those other women into the bed with him. His wife can feel it, sense it; she knows it. Sin does not belong in a believer's life. The marriage bed is undefiled in all things... as long as the only participants are a husband and wife! 'Nuff said about that.

We suggest that a man listen to his wife's heart in order to become the man that God has called him to be. In light of this we have to speak directly to the ladies about "Adventures in Lovemaking!" We have discovered that in a number of Christian marriages the wife is not comfortable participating in giving and receiving pleasure in varied sexual expressions. Only the most basic form of lovemaking is acceptable. This aversion may stem from sexual experiences that she had before she was a believer. Another possibility is that she may have been sexually abused as a child.

Statistics say that approximately 50% of women were sexually abused at some point in childhood. This is the world we live in. A woman who was sexually abused as a child can be plagued with flashbacks during lovemaking. Sadly, lovemaking becomes a 'trigger' for horrible memories for some victims. It would be totally normal for this wife to go from "extremely interested" to "no interest" in a flash. She cannot help this. She is still being victimized by the abuse.

God calls us as men to be agents of healing for our wives. Not agents of further emotional pain. A woman should express her heart to her man regularly and he will grow by responding to his wife's needs in kindness, gentleness and love. As you are sensitive and supportive, your wife will be seeking a total healing in her memories. She does not **want** to be attacked in her mind when you are making love. She did not **volunteer** to be abused as a child. She knows that it is not God's will for you as a couple to miss out on the full pleasures that married lovemaking offers. In these sensitive circumstances, it may take a while to reach a place of full expression in lovemaking, but you will arrive. *"You have need of patience, so that after you have done the will of God, you may receive the promise" Hebrews 10:36.* A little bit out of context, but it applies to this circumstance.

What has been our main theme throughout this book? God gave you the perfect wife with the perfect needs for you to meet. You will become the man that God has called you to become when you are successfully meeting your wife's needs. As you are sensitive to your wife and place a premium value on her feelings, she will begin to heal and over time she will respond as you desire.

IF A HUSBAND IS CHANGING INTO THE MAN GOD HAS CALLED HIM TO BE, THEN WONDERFUL THINGS ARE HAPPENING. HE IS BECOMING MORE SENSITIVE, GENTLE AND KIND.

In other cases, some wives may just be personally opposed to anything except for very basic lovemaking. The marriage manual in a wife's heart can be a trusted guide to follow **unless** her manual is signaling a message that is not supported by the Word.

A quality husband can live with a few years of lack in some areas of his sex life with his wife if she is truly being healed of serious emotional harm that was done to her as a child. On the other hand, it is an **invalid** application of our teaching for a wife to use it to defend not participating in adventurous lovemaking simply because it is a new experience.

A man also had dreams of what married life was going to be like before he was married; lots of variety in lovemaking topped his list.

There are some very interesting verses in the Song of Solomon. They describe lovemaking as an exciting adventure of exploration and discovery.

> *I sat down in his shade with great delight and his*
> *fruit was sweet to my taste.*
>
> *Song of Solomon 2:3b*

> *While the King is at his table, my spikenard sends*
> *forth its fragrance.*
>
> *Song of Solomon 1:12*

> *Blow upon my garden that its spices may flow out.*
> *Let my beloved come to his garden and eat its*
> *pleasant fruits.*
>
> *Song of Solomon 4:16*

If one spouse wants to be more adventurous in the bedroom but this desire is unfulfilled the marriage is unwittingly set up for problems. The rejected spouse will be living with a sense of disappointment. He or she will not be able to enjoy the fulfillment of the honorable, legitimate and scriptural marital desire for a love life that is full of variety and spice!

Occasionally, we meet a **husband** who refuses to initiate lovemaking. His wife expressed a need for sex early in the marriage and he refused. He has regularly denied her ever since. The man who denies his wife sex is no different than the man who refuses to express love and affirmation to his wife in other ways. He is simply refusing to meet her need. Why? Because he knows she *needs* it to feel emotionally validated and satisfied! This is not a deep psychological issue. It is selfishness. Nothing more. Nothing less. His wife wants to make love. She wants the closeness and affirmation it represents. Maybe she just has a strong sex drive. He is refusing to meet her need. Plain and simple. It is not a problem with performance. This man normally self-gratifies with pornography. The issue is that he refuses to meet his individual wife's needs. Grow up. Meet your wife's need. Issue solved.

I, Joel, do not have authority over my body. Kathy does! **My body is hers!** From the tip of my head to the soles of my feet! My eyes, my ears, my toes, my kneecaps and everything in between are hers!

I, Kathy, do not have authority over **my** body! Joel does! **My body is his!** From the tip of my head to the souls of my feet! My eyes, my ears, my toes, my kneecaps and everything in between are his! This arrangement keeps our life fun, spontaneous and *very* interesting!

The Bible states that God has put His **Word** above His **name. He** freely **chose** to **submit His omnipotent power** to the **confines of His Word!** If **our conscience** feels violated by something that the **Word approves of** then we have to let the **Word** be the **final authority.** The **Word of God cannot** be **subservient** to **our** conscience.

Your sex life should not be hindered by a faulty conscience! Commit this verse to memory:

> *Marriage is honorable among all and the bed undefiled...*
>
> *Hebrews 13:4a*

This verse, in combination with the other passages that we have referred to already in this chapter let you know that your creator created lovemaking to be enjoyed often, enthusiastically and with variety. If your **heart** condemns you**, God is greater than your heart.** Ask Him to heal you of any aversion that you may have to any form of lovemaking. God knows that you have a problem with this. He knows all things and **He does not condemn you,** so **do not let your heart** condemn you!

> *For **if our heart condemns us, God is greater than our heart,** and knows all things.*
> 1 John 3:20

LOVEMAKING SHOULD BE THE EASIEST PART OF MARRIED LIFE!

Dr. Kevin Leman shared a story in his book, *Sheet Music,* which I found to be extremely funny! He was watching the aged and beloved Charlie Shedd on a Christian talk show. Charlie Shedd is the universally loved, now deceased author of the best selling classics, *Letters to Phillip* and *Letters to Karen.* His books have sold over 8 million copies!

Dr. Leman shares that another guest on the program was describing how hot hell would be for any Christian who decided to participate in some various forms of creative (oral) lovemaking. After expressing his *opinions* as to why Christians were forbidden to enjoy God's gift in all of the ways that a married couple is able, he paused. The host asked Charlie what he thought about the man's position. Charlie simply said, "Hey, don't knock it 'til you try it!" The rabid preacher's face went pale! Blame Charlie, not us! Sometimes it takes an ancient one to gently bring the Body of Christ back into the truth. We are just reporting what Charlie said, as recorded in Dr. Leman's book! (smile) If a married couple will just decide that sex is fun, if they will determine that **"more** is good" and if they will pursue a variety in time, place and style, many marital frustrations will vanish!

It is amazing to see how much a marriage improves when the couple can spend a lot of time in bed. Frank and Kathy Lee Gifford came through their public humiliation successfully. Kathy had praised Frank on national TV as the perfect husband. Suddenly he was caught in a hotel room with someone other than her. This was a national incident. They had to respond to each other while the entire nation waited to see what would happen.

One key to their restoration was their counselor's suggestion that they spend as much time as possible **naked in bed** for the next 30 days! They did so with wonderful results! This would be fun, but if a husband is not working and the couple is not independently wealthy like Frank and Kathy Lee then he cannot ask his wife to spend the day in bed. He needs to be looking for a job! Get a job and provide financial security. **Then** you can enjoy that full day of lovemaking!

Stress contributes to the loss of interest in sex for many women. **If your wife is stressed,** make it **your** priority to lift her load and diminish her stress, thus increasing the potential for great sex! Contributing factors to stress include a new job, a new house, marital discord, a new church, financial pressures, the loss of friends, family or loved ones, fractured relationships and other like issues.

Don't get angry with your wife if her level of interest in sex is low. Eliminate her stress!

Additional words of caution to a husband who is recovering from being a control-freak:

- Sex is designed by God to be fun and a true pleasure for both spouses in giving and receiving.

- You do own your wife's body, but a normal guy realizes that this does not mean that she has to jump when he barks. Recovering control-freaks are in the process of learning what boundaries are. Let your wife tell you if she is feeling pressured.

Their marriage was in crisis. Tom wanted to make love. Bonnie wanted him to work on the house. Making a few repairs - which had been put off for a year - would be a message that he cared for Bonnie and their ten-year-old child. Bonnie would feel secure – and then be happy to make love. A wise and loving man would have worked on that house! Tom was not wise... **or** loving. He refused to "give in." The last we heard, Tom was homeless and jobless, living out of the trunk of his car. Bonnie hired a handy-man. She and her ten-year-old are doing just fine.

- Be happy with "quickies" when your wife is not in the mood. If your wife ever complains that you are being too rough or causing her discomfort, buy and read the three books we recommended earlier.

243

- A man operating in the love of God will not ask his partner to be subjected to undesirable physical pain. A man who insists that his wife submit to physical pain would be guilty of sexual abuse. Sex is designed to be a pleasure to both.

Our goal has been to take the brakes off of sex in your married life. We have presented some adventurous attitudes and freedom-inducing thought. If your marriage is enhanced as a result then we have succeeded. We have balanced our suggestions with some warnings designed to create a protective buffer for wives of recovering control freaks. If a husband **will heed the warnings** and if his wife **will take the brakes off** then this can be a huge step toward experiencing that dream marriage.

**You sir, can be the *man* of her dreams
and you, ma'am, can be the *woman* of his!**

Turn the heat up!

You can **start** now.

Ahem. We're *waiting*...

GOLDEN KEY

JUST SAY YES...
TO TURNING UP THE HEAT!